Grateful Testimonials

"We just got this exact e-mail from Frenza Hollis, we are an art publishing business and they must have gotten our e-mails from our website. Thank you for posting this as a scam, we may have had to learn the hard way, because we do get legitimate inquiries from other countries occasionally."

"WOW thank you very much for informing me about this!!! This person just contacted me and said the same exact thing!! I knew it was too good to be true. I almost got scammed but thanks to you I did not! Please stop these disgusting people."

"Just got the letter wanting about $30,000 worth of art to be paid by credit card by Mary James but they want me to contact their shippers in Malaysia. Thanks for posting this and saving me a lot of time tracking this down as another scam."

"Hi. I wanted to say thanks for taking the time to post this online. I just got contacted by this person and googled his phone # only to find your blog with all the emails/responses similar to the ones I've received. Needless to say I won't be spending any more time on him. Much appreciated!"

"Dear Kathleen, thank you for your art scam website. I found the perpetrator "Mark Peters" listed as another scammer. He/She recently contacted me to sell 56 fan veils, all shipped to the Philippines. Thank you for having a site like this, it really helped me stay clear of a criminal!"

"Dear Kathleen, I am sure I am receiving e-mails from a scammer calling themselves Angela Howard. I searched the web for info and came up with your name, website, etc. I did send the person my address and phone number but will now cease communications. Very grateful for your information and efforts to bring attention to this. Thank you!"

"Thanks for posting this—it has saved me a lot of time and $!! Mine was from Joy at the david email address. I googled the email address and found myself here. THANK YOU!!!"

Hi Kathleen: Thanks so much for compiling this information! You really saved me hours of aggravation.

"Thanks, a friend of mine just received a similar mail with some different locations, etc. Again, thank you very much for your fight!"

"I'm an artist in Massachusetts and was hit by Ruby/Sofia/David Howard, just wanted to let you know I filed a complaint and I really appreciate your work in providing the information."

*Thank you Katie, you are indeed a Samurai in the war against lame #@!!*** scammers.*

Top 10 Email Scams

Detect & Protect Yourself from Online Scams

Volume 1 of the

Internet Scams Revealed Series

Kathleen McMahon

Disclaimer: The information I have written in this book is solely intended to provide a general understanding of the subject matter and to help readers assess whether they need to seek more detailed information. The material in this publication is not and must not be regarded as legal advice. Readers should seek their own legal advice where appropriate. I have endeavored to make sure that the information contained herein is accurate, however no liability is accepted for any loss or damage whatsoever that can be attributed to the reliance on any of that information.

Publisher: KTMObooks, 1450 Chestnut Street #102, San Francisco, CA 94123

ISBN: 978-1-938831-00-3

Library of Congress Control Number: 2012914606

This book is dedicated to all the victims of email scams, so that there may be fewer of you in which to dedicate this book..

Contents

INTRODUCTION

Sometimes it feels like me against the enormous invisible endless sea of Internet scammers. I know this is not true. I know I am not alone. But sometimes it feels that way.

Internet scammers came into my life really at the very beginning of the Internet. I was on the band wagon from the first day. In fact, I was the first woman SYSOP in California on a system that pre-dated the Internet, called rBBSnet. It was kind of a store-and-forward system for email. We thought it was lightning fast at the time. I laugh about it now. Good times. But not so fast times by any means.

As someone who has had a technical life since 1983, it was natural that people would turn to me when the Internet days took off, like so many fireworks, to figure out if the emails they were getting were for "real". It took a while for the scammers to really get with the idea that the Internet was going to be their new frontier, but once they did, it was like cockroaches entering a whole new dreamy yummy environment - and to one degree or another, they were never going to leave ever again. They are adaptable buggers.

I've been happy to help people figure out scam emails - in "guestbooks" in the early days, on AOL chat rooms (oh, how I date myself!), in forum message boards. Then one day not that long ago, I got 5 emails in one day from fellow artists who had all lost between $1000-$5000 each to scammers, writing to me too late, and it hit me all at one time - how many emails had I received over the years? 5,000? 10,000? more?

I realized it was time to do something on a larger scale.

The authorities weren't going to do anything. Scammers love to stay under the radar and in countries where it is hard to prosecute them. I knew that scammers were using the Internet to pretty much get a huge number of victims for literally no cost (quite an improvement over the old days of actually having to send some kind of mailer through the postal system or make an actual phone call). So I decided I would use the Internet as they do, by bringing their emails, their activities, and the nature of their scams out into the light - post them publicly, get others to post what they receive, have it all show up in search results. Then people just need to learn to search online BEFORE sending any money to anyone, or giving up personal financial information or passwords. That's the plan. The Anti-Scam Samurai Plan. Slash them with light.

And so my life as an Anti-Scam Samurai began. I encourage people online and we post everything we can. I started by helping friends, clients, and artists - they are my "people", but a scam is a scam is a scam and scammers don't really care who they target, so my efforts have expanded beyond helping artists.

At first, I began a list of scammer names and email addresses on my art website. Scammers fake all their names and use disposable email addresses but I still wanted to make this list so it would show up in search results if someone was searching on it, and confirm for that user that it was indeed a scam. I wanted more interactivity, so I started a blog, called Stop Art Scams (stopartscams.blogspot.com). I post scams that people send me and everyone jumps in on the comments and share their experiences related to that scam. It all shows up in search results. It really has helped a lot of people avoid becoming scam victims. I felt good about that but not so great about continuing to receive emails from people who had actually lost money to scammers. So next I opened a page, also called Stop Art Scams, on Facebook (http://www.facebook.com/pages/Stop-Art-Scams/135887239769963). Even more scam information shows up in search results. Yea! Even though it says Stop Art Scams, we really do welcome all Internet scam posts to share.

And now I realized I really *do* need to expand beyond helping artists and reach even more people. I want to make the life of an Internet scammer as difficult as possible. So now I've written a series of books to spread the word to more people and hopefully continue to reduce the number of scam victims.

The first book in the series, Volume 1, is called *Top 10 Email Scams*. It describes each scam, how they work, how to recognize them, and how to avoid them. It also provides information on what to do if you do become a victim, and how to deal with (and avoid) identity theft. The second volume covers the scams that are prevalent on the social media platforms, such as Craigslist, eBay, Facebook, Twitter, etc. Volume 2 is called *Social Media Scams*. A supplemental resource guide, called *Report Scams*, provides links and contact information for victims of Internet scams. I will be releasing more topics in this series. The whole series is called *Internet Scams Revealed*. You can sign up for my free newsletter at my website to be kept updated on releases.

To support the book series and provide an additional space to share scam experiences, there is another Blog (KTMObooks.com/blog/), another Facebook page (facebook.com/KTMObooks), and a Twitter account (twitter.com/KTMObooks). I'm going to cast the information net far and wide. My goal is to educate,

educate, educate, and see if all of these efforts will have a growing impact on lowering the number of people finding themselves victim to Internet scams.

Take out your swords. Let's continue to make Internet scammers scramble and work harder at their crimes. Let's shine a light on them. Welcome to the battle.

- Kathleen

CHAPTER 1
THE BASICS OF A SCAM

There are many Internet scam variations in existence but they all have several basic components which enable them to be successful. These basic structural parts often remain surprisingly consistent. Let's take a look at the basic elements of a scam and a little more about who scammers are.

What is a Scam?

The most basic definition of a scam is when someone obtains money or sensitive information from someone else using deception. On the internet, scammers make use of the technology to reach the maximum number of potential victims for the least amount of cost – typically no cost at all. Sending emails has proven to be the most effective means scammers can use to lure in their victims.

All scams have four basic components. The stories and the approaches will change but they all include these four parts:

1. *The Story* – all of the stories contain the element of the scammer pretending to be someone they are not.

2. *The Mark* – scammers seek out the vulnerable, be it vulnerable people or vulnerable systems. With people, the scammer will appeal to the emotions of the person and then use their "story" to make themselves appear to be legitimate.

3. *Get In-Get Out* – all scammers want to get in, steal your money or information, and get out quickly, so all scams will contain some element of urgency. It is also beneficial to the scammer if they can get their victim to act before they realize what is happening or have time to consider the appropriateness of their actions.

4. *The Cash-Out* – all scams need to be able to cash out in a way that the scammer can not be tracked down after the money or financial information has been stolen.

Scam Alert Flags

Look for the Scam Alert Flags throughout the book. These are important clues that will assist you in quickly recognizing when an email is a scam, BEFORE you give up information or money. This is the key to reducing the success rate of any given scam.

Global Scam Volume

According to Radicati Group Inc. (http://www.radicati.com/), a California-based tech research group, it was estimated that in 2010 the number of emails sent per day was around 294 billion. 294 billion messages per day means more than 2.8 million emails were sent every second and some 90 trillion emails sent that year. Around 90% of those messages were spam, scams and viruses. The genuine emails sent that year were only around 1.9 billion. And that was in 2010. By 2013, Radicati Inc. forecasts approximately 507 billion e-mail messages will be sent each day.

In 2010, one Russian spammer was shut down and the overall spam level was instantly reduced by 20%. So while the problem of email spam and scams is widespread, it probably remains true that 20% of the spammers and scammers are responsible for 80% of the email traffic generated, if not more.

The Kaspersky Labs (http://www.kaspersky.com/), a Russian security firm, released this report in April 2012 stating that:

- March to April 2012 saw the spam percentage in email traffic went up 2.2 percentage points and averaged 77.2%.

- Phishing email percentages remained unchanged from

March 2012 and amounted to 0.01%.

- 2.8% of all emails contained malicious files in them, the same amount as March 2012.
- Facebook users comprised over 20% of phishing attacks in April 2012.

Who Are the Scammers?

Keep in mind that scammers work very hard to stay in the shadows. They don't want anyone, particularly their victims and the authorities, to know who they are. So they create false identities online including their name, gender, email address, photo, etc. Everything is made up. They steal the photo of some beautiful woman and put that on some fake profile and pretend that it is their own profile. Whether they themselves are a man or woman doesn't matter. They set up disposable email addresses under made-up names and when these accounts get shut down, they just set up another. These are often done at services like Gmail, Hotmail, and Yahoo.

Research still shows that 95% of scammers are typically young men, teenagers, and students. This is not always the case but mostly true. They also tend to come from countries where it would be hard for the authorities to track them down and prosecute them. That is why Nigeria has become so well known as a source of online scammers. While Nigeria has the public reputation, more recently online scammers have actually been coming from other countries. According to *Internet Fraud Watch* (http://www.fraud.org/), the countries where most internet fraud originate from are, in order: Ukraine, Indonesia, Yugoslavia, Lithuania, Egypt, Romania, Turkey, Russia, Pakistan, Malaysia, Israel and Nigeria. While it is true that India and China have been in the news for their advanced computer hacking skills, they do not currently make the list for where most online scams originate.

This is going to sound a bit judgemental but, for the most part, scammers pretty much look like scammers. If you ever end up seeing their actual photos (not an easy thing to do), you'll see what I am saying. They seem to look exactly like their behavior and moral character would suggest. There are entertaining websites out there which are known as "scam baiters". More vigilante in nature than I am, the people behind these sites trick the scammers back at their own scam, making them look silly and do ridiculous things and then photograph themselves (all on the hope of getting their money in the scam). They seem to be able to get many of these criminals to hold up funny signs of which the scammers do not appear to understand what the signs say.

Scam baiting is done more for sport and doesn't really advance the cause of reducing the number of victims, though it does clearly make scammers frustrated and mad once they realize they have jumped through all these weird hoops and still will not be getting their scammed money.

Here are a few examples of scammers who have been 'scam-baited':

I would not recommend participating in this activity unless you really know what you are doing. It could have some unanticipated consequences if the scammer were able to locate you and/or your email account, web server, etc.

I also had a regular reader of my Stop Art Scams blog stumble into the real photo of a scammer he was interacting with on Skype and here is the scammer's photo:

This scammer was operating under a fake woman's name of Anna Johnson.

Here are two women, a mother/daughter team, indicted recently for working with Nigerians who were posing as U.S. Military personnel on dating sites and stole over $1 million dollars from 374 unsuspecting women victims (see how profitable it is to be a scammer?), thinking they were helping the military men retrieve property, travel to the U.S., and pay other expenses. These two women would, according to the indictment, receive the stolen money, keep 10% and send the rest on to their associates in Nigeria as well as other foreign destinations. While I'm glad they were caught and indicted, they were just moving the money and the real profiteers were the Nigerians. The authorities still have not found an effective way to go after the source of the problem. And the scammers know it.

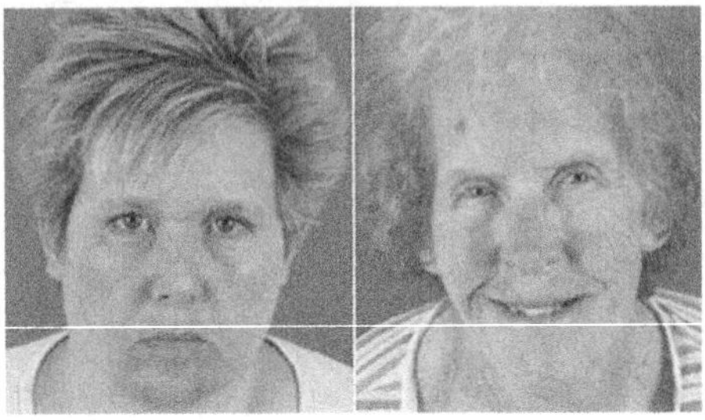

I suggest you do not feel bad for the scammer. They have hurt many innocent people. It is a common misconception from potential victims that scammers care what you say to them. They do not. They do not care to hear that you figured out it was a scam (though as soon as they know, they will disappear and move their attention on to other potential victims). They don't even care if you tell them you've called the authorities. They know it is unlikely they'll be caught. They don't care. Do not feel compelled to communicate any further with a scammer once you have figured out it is a scam. Just delete the email(s) and move on to the more important matters of your life.

Also keep in mind that scammers lie about EVERYTHING. Everything. Do not believe a single word a scammer says. They are not capable of telling the truth, and this includes scammers who threaten to show up at your door if you don't send the money. They will tell you they are moving from one country to another. They aren't. They will tell you their child is sick and needs money. They don't have a child and no one is sick. They will tell you that you have won the lottery. You haven't. They will tell you your bank account has a problem. It doesn't. They will tell you they represent two orphanages and need money. They don't. They will tell you they are a woman. They are not. Scammers lie. About everything. Have I made my point?

How Do Scammers Get Your Email Address?

It can seem incomprehensible that scammers can send out so many emails, often hundreds of thousands of them a day. Where do they get all these email addresses from? How did they find *your* email address?

There are six basic ways scammers collect up email addresses:

1. Scammers buy illegal lists of email addresses

Hackers will break into ISPs (Internet Service Providers) and other supposedly secured sources of email addresses and collect them up and sell them to scammers and spammers for good money.

2. Scammers use harvesting software programs

This is pretty common. There are many software programs being used by scammers and spammers that automatically scour the internet looking for any email addresses they can find publicly posted (and close variations, like jane doe @ yahoo.com, with the spaces). Surprisingly, there are a huge number of people who still post their email address publicly on forums, facebook, websites, and blogs, leaving themselves vulnerable.

3. Scammers use "dictionary" type of software to guess email addresses

This is also common. Their software generates untold number of combinations of letters and numbers at various typical ISP addresses, like Gmail.com, Yahoo.com, Hotmail.com, AOL.com, etc. Of course, many of these guesses will turn out to be invalid email addresses but a scammer doesn't care—he isn't sending those millions of emails out on his dime. He is typically hijacking someone else's server for that and making that server owner pay for the bandwidth of the emails being sent out as well as the bad emails bouncing back. Enough of these email addresses will actually be valid and go through to potential victims. It's a numbers game for the scammer.

4. Scammers use dishonest mailing lists

Scammers will sometimes use one of the methods above to collect up a large number of email addresses and then send out a fake newsletter with a link to unsubscribe. But for all the people who do unsubscribe—they are then confirmed as a valid email address and active user. The scammer can then sell that for more money than unevaluated email addresses. Or they will use it themselves but then can send a more targeted message to those people.

5. Scammers target large sources of users

In this case, the scammer has more work on his hands but he can then also send a more targeted scam message and hopefully (in his mind) have a higher percentage of successful victims. With this strategy, a scammer will manually send a targeted message to a smaller but more select niche of users. Online gathering places of a large number of users can be found at Craigslist, Facebook, and eBay. When scammers are targeting artists, I've seen them write a scam email to every member of an art association from their website (as long as members have links to their websites and from there email addresses to contact). Artists have also been targeted at Art.com, FineArtAmerica.com, and Etsy.com.

6. Scammers pretend to sell something great

In this case, scammers will make use of places online where they can post something for sale at no charge, like Craigslist. They will put an amazing price on some non-existent item with pretty broad appeal, and collect up the email addresses of all who reply to the ad. I've seen this done with job ads as well.

So How Can You Protect Your Email Address?

- Don't post your email publicly on the internet anywhere! I can't emphasize this enough.

- Disguise your email address on your website and blog using obfuscation or encryption so spammers can not suck it up into their databases.

- Use a disposable email address.

- Avoid confirming an "unsubscribe" request from a newsletter you do not know. Simply delete the email.

In the next chapter, we will review the top 10 most common email scams in more depth.

CHAPTER 2
TOP 10 EMAIL SCAMS

1. 419 Nigerian Advanced Fee Scam

This remains one of the most popular and successful scams on the Internet. This originates out of Nigeria and has been named the 419 scam after the section of the Nigerian penal code which addresses fraud schemes, but now these emails can be found coming from other countries as well. Lots of people look at these emails and say it is so obvious that they are a scam, but unfortunately many people continue to be enticed into believing they are either going to come into a lot of money or can make money for basically doing very little. The scammer also devises documents with official-looking mastheads and photographs so the victim might believe this proves the scammer's story is for real.

How It Works

These schemes work by getting the victim engaged in a long detailed story promising to share a very large sum of money for "helping them", then supporting that story by presenting, in various steps, forged documents, on-going made-up communications, and in some rare cases even convincing the victim to come visit the country for meetings with officials, which are all staged.

At the crucial point of the scam, the scammers will ask the victim to advance them money to pay sudden fees or bribes to keep the deal going. They will continue to wring the victim of as much money as possible. They may even ask for additional money just to keep the victim included in the "opportunity". Once the scammers believe they have pretty much gotten all they the cash they can from the victim, they disappear. The victim may also then have their identity stolen if they have already provided lots of personal and sensitive information.

The scammers use a variety of stories to explain why they need the victim's help to access the funds (funds which are really non-existent). For example:

- The scammer will describe in great details how some political or legal situation prevents them from accessing funds in the foreign bank account where the money sits.

- The scammer will conveniently suggest you have the same last name as the dead person with the big bucks and suggest that you can act as the Next of Kin of in order to gain access to the funds and share a portion of it with them.

- The scammer use the angle of claiming to be a wealthy

merchant and they are soon dying of a terrible terminal disease and seeking your assistance to distribute his or her wealth to charity, again on the promise to share a portion of it with you.

It has been a curiosity to me why in these emails the scammers are so upfront about saying they are from Nigeria when so many people know emails from Nigeria are scams. But then I came upon an enlightening paper.

Microsoft researcher Cormac Herley wrote the paper, *Why do Nigerian scammers say they are from Nigeria?* (http://research.microsoft.com/pubs/167719/WhyFromNigeria.pdf) in which he posed an interesting question: Why DO Nigerian scammers admit they are from Nigeria? His answer is pretty simple and goes to show how a scammer's mind works: scammers don't want anyone but the most gullible – and therefore the most likely to follow through – to respond to the emails because it costs scammers time, money, and effort to continue past the first email. The point for the Nigerian scammer is to weed out those who will back out with the initial email, and then to focus their effort on those more likely to fall for the entire scheme.

He also made the point that it is counter intuitive to wanting to end the communication immediately, but the best way to make a scammer "pay" is to use up their time knowing you are never going to send them any money.

Of course, I always caution people to be careful about messing with scammers – if they get pissed off enough they have the option to start attacking your email account, your website, your server, etc. Often it is just not worth it in the long run, but my point here is do not feel bad about stringing the scammer along just a little bit if you want to do so.

So, to summarize the 419 Nigerian Advancced Fee Scam, if you discover an email in your in-box proposing a complicated arrangement to secure and split funds from a foreign country, you can safely assume someone is trying to trap you into a 419 scam.

Scam Alert Flags

- long complicated story involving foreign country and/or foreign dignitary

- they are the beneficiary or are seeking the surviving beneficiaries

- banking particulars are requested from the victim

- the scammer emphasizes how confidential the transaction needs to be

- unrealistically high amounts of money

– call for urgent response

EXAMPLE EMAIL:

```
Return-path: [philipamos@mail.kz]

Received: from [197.251.144.255] (account
philipamos@mail.kz)  by backend01n.mail.kz
(CommuniGate Pro WEBUSER 5.2.13)

From: "philip amos" (philipamos@mail.kz)

Subject:  A  FRIEND  OFFER

X-Mailer: CommuniGate Pro WebUser v5.2.13

Message-ID: (web-78247594@backend01n.mail.kz)

Dear Friend,

This message might meet you in utmost
surprise. However, it's just my urgent need
for foreign partner that made me to contact
you. My name is Philip Amos son of late
Lt.eulud Benson Alafia who was murdered on 15
march at Tripoli Intelligence Compound, the
problem (war) in my country which have already
claim the life of thousand as such I am
running away with the remaining family out of
(Tripoli) Libya.

Nevertheless, I have the sum of $11.5 million
that was concealed in a Two Trunk Boxes and
deposited with a Private Security Company in
the Republic of Ghana and I herein need
someone like you to assist me by standing as
the Owner and Beneficiary of the
aforementioned Fund.

I will give you 15% out of the total cash.
Please Keep it secret as we want to come there
and live quietly without people noticing that
```

```
we have come with huge fortune. I have also
map out 5% for charity.

Remember your reply will help the family along
way.

Thanks

Philip Amos
```

Often scammers will not reveal very much in their first email, which gets sent to millions of people. As mentioned, they then can focus their attention on just those people who reply to the first inquiry. Now they have a pool of interested responders who are potential victims, worthy of putting more of their effort into the rest of the scam. They move on to the next step of the scam with these people. Here is an example of a "first" email (notice how the 'FROM' email is ahwoikwesi11@gmail.com, but the 'REPLY-TO' email is slightly different ahwoi.kwesi@yahoo.com and the scammer has hijacked the use of the tce.edu servers).

EXAMPLE EMAIL:

```
Return-path: [ahwoikwesi11@gmail.com]

Received: from [127.0.0.1] (helo=mail.tce.edu)

Subject: Waiting to hear from you

From: "Hon. Kwesi Ahwoi"
[ahwoikwesi11@gmail.com]

Reply-To: ahwoi.kwesi@yahoo.com

I have a business for you to handle with me.
```

Should you be interested,

Kindly contact me via (ahwoi.kwesi@yahoo.com) for more details.

Thanks

Hon. Kwesi Ahwoi

+233543146547

This email was sent using TCEMail Service.

Thiagarajar College of Engineering

Madurai-625 015, India

If you search online on the phrase "Thiagarajar College of Engineering" you will see both legitimate references but also references to other scam emails sent from these servers.

Below is yet another example where the scammer tries to prey on people who feel sorry for their woe-is-me story.

EXAMPLE EMAIL:

From: MRS. MARYLIN SHARON WALLANCE (mrsmarilynsharon@yahoo.com.ph)

Dearly Beloved,

I'm Mrs.Marylin Sharon Wallance resident in Lancashire, Western province of England in the UK suffering from cancerous ailment. I was married to Sir Raymond Jeremy Cassel Sharon an English based shipping tycoon notable for his great wealth, influential extended family and charitable activities all his life before his death. My husband died after a protracted illness in April 5th, 2009. Our life together as husband and wife lasted for about two and a half decades without a child.

My late husband and I made a vow to uplift the down-trodden and the less-privileged individuals in the society, as we both had passion for those people who cannot help themselves due to physical disability or financial predicament. I can adduce the fact that, we needed a Child from our marriage which never came. When my late husband was alive he invested in stocks the sum of Thirteen Million United States dollars ($13,500,000.00), which he derived from his vast investment in capital market with a Company here in the UK and named me as the sole beneficiary of this trust funds upon his demise.

Just last week, my Doctor told me that I have limited days to live, due to the cancerous problems that I have been suffering from. What bothers me most is the stroke that I have in addition with the cancer. With the hard reality that has befallen me, I have decided to donate the funds to you and I want you to use the gift which comes from my late husband effort to establish a charitable Foundation called "Cassel Charity Foundation" for the upkeep of widows, orphans, destitute, the down- trodden, physically challenged children, barren-women and persons who prove to be genuinely handicapped financially around you, as it is often said that blessed is the hand that giveth.

I took the bold decision to contact you, because I do not have any child to inherit the money and my late husband relatives are bourgeois and very wealthy persons that will misuse and invest the money into ill perceived ventures if willed to them, instead of helping the poor in a worthy manner.

I do not need any telephone communication in this regard, due to my deteriorating health and the presence of my husband relatives around me, as I am currently bedridden in my husband Family house here in Lancashire, England and do not receive any visitors unless approved by my late husband immediate younger brother and I do not want him and the rest of the family members to know about this development, in order to safeguard this bequest.

My happiness today is that I lived a life worthy of emulation and I want you to be kindhearted all through your life. Please, send me the follow details:

YOUR FULL NAME.

CONTACT ADDRESS.

COUNTRY.

CELL PHONE NUMBER.

AGE/SEX.

OCCUPATION.

With Love,

Mrs.Marylin Sharon Wallance.

mrsmarylinsharon@aol.com

2. Credit Card/Loan Advanced Fee Scam

This scam looks like an official offer from a credit card company or lending bank to send you a "pre-approved" credit card or loan for an upfront fee. Given how hard it is these days to get loans, many victims believe if they just pay the fee they can secure that loan or credit card that otherwise they would not have qualified for through normal channels. They are hoping it is a back door to getting a loan or credit card. The scammers are also hoping people just won't take the time to really read the fine-print of the offer or check out the bank or credit card company through other sources.

There is no credit card offer nor is there a pre-approved loan. There is just a scammer there ready to take your upfront fee and disappear.

When dealing with legitimate credit card companies, many charge annual fee, but it is applied after you have the card, to the balance of your account. Scammers are hoping you don't know this fact and charge their "fee" upfront before you get the card. Pre-approved loan offer can NOT be legitimate if the loan company knows nothing about your credit situation.

Scam Alert Flags

– pre-approved credit card offer containing an upfront fee

– pre-approved loan without knowing your credit details

– a lender using a similar sounding or "copy-cat" name

– a lender not registered in your state

– a lender who never checks your credit history, yet asks for your personal information, such as your Social Security number or bank account number

– urgency to act now or miss the offer

– upfront fee requested via wire transfer, such as Western Union

This was a notice posted on the website of the Attorney General of Maine and illustrates how this scam worked in this one case:

August 19, 2010

Contact: Maine Attorney General (207) 626-8599

Attorney General Janet T. Mills warns of a new "advance fee" credit card fraud that is targeting Maine residents. Southern Maine's PeoplesChoice Credit Union reports that scammers have been claiming to be from "PeoplesChoice Saving" and offering a credit card with a $2000 line of credit. In return the callers ask for payment of $200 and the victim's bank account information so they can immediately withdraw the funds from the victim's account. Brenda Piecuch, Compliance Manager and Information Security Officer for PeoplesChoice Credit Union, says that they "have received 25 calls over the past three weeks from people who have been contacted by the scammers. PeoplesChoice Credit Union has nothing to do with this illegal offer." PeoplesChoice has branches in Biddeford, Wells, Saco and Sanford." Advance Fee Credit Card scams are fraudulent and prey on people who desperately need a line of credit.

Mills warns consumers never to give out bank account or other personal identifying information over the telephone or over the Internet without confirming the identity and address of the requestor. "Verify. Verify. Verify," Mills said, "and never send money to people you don't know. No legitimate bank doing business in Maine will ask you for money or account information over the phone or over the Internet."

3. Lottery Scam

Lottery scams are really successful online and utilize a version of the advanced-fee scam where a person sends money, sometimes pitched as taxes or a processing fee to a claims agent, in anticipation of receiving lottery winning – for a lottery they have never entered.

How It Works:

An email will arrive saying you've won a lottery, often in a foreign country or you have been randomly selected to receive a prize. That is all the first email will typically reveal. The scammer is waiting to proceed only with those people who reply to the email because then the scammer has a pool of potential victims who are pre-disposed to going all the way through the scam. On the replies, the scammer will then explain the next stage, which is to describe the winnings in more detail and then throw in – almost as an after thought, that there is a fee in order to collect the winnings. Or the scammer might try and collect your personal information first and then go for the fee, so even if you become suspicious about the fee, they've already taken a bunch of your personal and sensitive information. And of course, the fee will eventually be requested via wire transfer because thet is the untraceable way scammers steal their money and disappear. There is no lottery and no prize. Unfortunately, many people fall for this scam because the scammer's communications seem legitimate or the victim is typically in dire need of the money and so is willing to take a chance on it.

Scam Alert Flags

– an email declaring you've won a lottery (or drawing) when you've never entered one

– official lottery organizations never do random drawings on people who have not purchased a ticket

– an email saying you've won, but the email address is not the domain name of a real organization but instead an email from a Hotmail, Yahoo, Gmail type of account instead (be careful of altered email headers, which may use an email from the organization but the REPLY-TO email is different and typically a web-based email address like Gmail or Yahoo)

– any email requiring you to pay any fees or taxes before receiving a prize of any sort. If your prize is for real, there are no fees, and taxes would be withheld before the money is awarded

EXAMPLE EMAIL:

```
Subject: The Irish Email Lottery Fund

The Irish Lottery

[Address Removed]

Dublin 1, Ireland

(Customer Services)

Ref: UK/9420X2/68

Batch: 074/05/ZY369
```

WINNING NOTIFICATION:

We happily announce to you the draw (#1004) of the IRISH LOTTERY online Sweepstakes International program held on [date inserted here]. It is now available for claims and you are getting the final NOTIFICATION as regards this.

Your e-mail address attached to ticket number:56475600545 188 with Serial number 5368/02 drew the lucky numbers:14, 19, 29, 32, 36, 39, (bonus no.18) which subsequently won you the lottery in the 2nd category i.e match 5 plus bonus.

You have therefore been approved to claim a total sum of £1,350,000(One million, three hundred and fifty thousand, pounds sterling) in cash credited to file KTU/9023118308/03. This is from a total cash prize of £4,419,864 shared amongst the(5)lucky winners in this category i.e Match 6 plus bonus.All participants for the online version were selected randomly from World Wide Web sites through computer draw system and extracted from over 100,000 unions, emails addresses,associations, and corporate bodies that are listed online. This promotion takes place weekly. Please note that your lucky winning number falls within our United Kingdom booklet representative office in United Kingodm as indicated in your play coupon. In view of this, your £1,350,000(One million, three hundred and fifty thousand, pounds sterling) will be released to you by any of our payment offices in United Kingdom. Our United Kingdom agent will immediately commence the process to facilitate the release of your funds as soon as you contact him.For security reasons, you are advised to keep your winning information confidential till your claim is processed and your money remitted to you in whatever manner you deem fit to claim your prize.

This is part of our precautionary measure to avoid double claiming and unwarranted abuse of this program. Please be warned!!!

To file for your claim, please contact our fiduciary agent below: Call Bar.Galvin Mayor (ESQ) for confirmation immediately.

BARRISTER GALVIN MAYOR

Alpha Consultants mayorfirm & Schmidtz Associates

(Solicitors Advocates & Arbitrators) [Phone numbers removed]

Official Email: galvinmayorr@yahoo.com.au

Fiduciary Agent/Payment Officer.

Endeavour to email/fax him your full names, winning numbers,email/billing address, telephone and fax numbers immediately.

Endeavour to email him the informations below:

VERIFICATION AND CLEARANCE FORM

1.FULL NAMES:----------------------------------

2.ADDRESS:------------------------------

3.SEX:----------------------------------

4.AGE:----------------------------------

5.MARITAL STATUS:-------------------------------

6.OCCUPATION:---------------------------

7.E-MAIL ADDRESS:

```
-----------------------------------------

8.TELEPHONE
NUMBER:-----------------------------------

9.BATCH
NUMBER:----------------------------------

10. REF
NUMBER:----------------------------------

11.BRIEF DESCRIPTION OF
COMPANY/INDIVIDUAL:--------------------

12.AMOUNT
WON:-------------------------------------

13. COUNTRY:------------------------------

Congratulations from me and members of staff
of THE IRISH LOTTERY.

Yours faithfully,

Mrs. Melissa Johnson

Online coordinator for THE IRISH LOTTERY

Sweepstakes International Program
```

Notice in the below email headers how the real originating point of the email is in Australia.

EXAMPLE EMAIL:

```
X-SID-PRA: euro_millions2@aol.com

Received: from User ([83.46.229.130]) by
mail.angelopo.com.au with Microsoft
SMTPSVC(6.0.3790.4675);

Reply-To:
[euromillionmillionseuroeuro@aol.com]
```

From: "Euro Millions"[euro_millions2@aol.com]

To:

Subject: Reference Nr.XKHL-37-14-29-13)

Return-Path: euro_millions2@aol.com

Message-ID:
[DC01AUSYDKBT12XTRWJ00000892@mail.angelopo.com.au]

Confirmation Ticket N?: 33-48-19-H5H-@WIN

Contact Person: Chris Lewis,

Reference Nr.XKHL-37-14-29-13), Batch N?. DFD-25-30-29-686H, Serial N. PMSQ021542311,Ticket N?:.33-48-19-H5H-@WIN, lucky N.4-19-26-27-30-3-8, You have won(1Million Euros)in the euromillions online sweepstaks program corporations, held on 31st of May 2012. In Madrid (SPAIN). This email was sent to notify you officially about the award and to advise you to contact the processing office immediately for claim, Reply to Email: euromillionmillionseuroeuro@aol.com

Sincerely,

Mrs Sarry Keithson

euromillionmillionseuroeuro@aol.com

And here is another example ('From' and 'Reply-To' addresses are different):

EXAMPLE EMAIL:

From: "Western.Union" [rytrul@cox.net]

Subject: winner!

```
Reply-To: wumt0@cafuc.net

Attention Our Dear Beneficiary, please be
informed that  $11 Million Dollars has been
deposited in our Western Union office and we
are instructed to transfer to you $11 Million
Dollars by the Commonwealth Lottery Board as
compesation Prize,Contact your claims agent Mr
John Gibbs via Email:

(wumt0@aol.com)
```

4. "Phishing" Scams

"Phishing" (pronounced 'fishing') is what is referred to when a scammer tricks you into providing them your personal and financially sensitive information, because you didn't realize the form you were filling out was not actually a legitimate form. When the email looks like it comes from your bank and says there is a problem and please click here to log in and reactivate your account, if you are not paying attention carefully, you'll not notice your actual bank has not written to you at all and there is nothing wrong with your banking account – this is how phishing works. The creators of these phishing scams design the fake website pages to look so much like the real web page that you don't even notice the difference (which may only be the actual URL and even that if often something that looks vaguely correct but is not).

When the scammers send out these phishing emails that

pretend to be from banks, they send it to everyone, knowing each person who has no account with that bank will immediately delete the email. But they are after those potential victims who DO have an account with that bank and so may click in the link and proceed to the fake page and fill out the information requested, thinking they are reactivating their online banking account.

Always be sure to check that the URL is a legitimate one for your bank and really, don't click on links in emails like this – go to your bank's website manually.

EXAMPLE EMAIL:

From: Bank of America [accounts@bankofamerica.com]

Subject: Please update your account information

Dear Bank of America Customer,

As a courtesy to our valued customer, Bank of America conducts regular account information verification processes. During the most recent process, we found that we could not verify your information.

In order to ensure your account information is not made vulnerable, please visit http://www.bankofamerica.accounts-update.com.

Please click on the above link to our Web site and confirm or update your account information. If you do not do this within 48 hours of receipt of this e-mail, you will not be able to use your Bank of America account

```
for 30 days. This is an extra precaution we
take to ensure your account remains secure.

Sincerely,

Bank of America Customer Service
```

Remember, these fake sites are hard to distinguish from the real legitimate website so always be cautious when being asked for personal information online, especially around banking information.

Scam Alert Flags

– an email claiming your bank or paypal account needs urgent attention

– an email declaring there is some problem with your account & requesting you provide financial or personal identity information

– an email alert that there is a problem with your shipment and the shipping company requires information to verify your identity

– the label of click link (what you visually see when reading the email) does not match the actual destination link when you mouse over it. Do not click on it

– in viewing the full email headers, the FROM and/or REPLY-TO are not from the organization or institution

Notice in the example that follows they've faked most of the header information so you think the return address is someone at Target.com. But the actual Reply-To address is different and sources to a server in Russian (ip number: 178.44.243.148).

EXAMPLE EMAIL:

```
From: Rose Duke [RoseDuke77231@gmail.com]

Return-path: [emily.reid@target.com]

Reply-To: [q3icky@rodman-tech.com]

Subject: Your Tax Payment ID: 01037733 has
been rejected. Urgent Report information.

Your Federal Tax Payment ID: 010375128 has
been rejected. Return Reason Code R21 - The
identification number used in the Company
Identification Field is not valid.

Please, check the information and refer to
Code R21 to get details about your company
payment in transaction contacts section:

http://eftps.gov/R21 [Links to
http://eftpsID55555.com/contacts/s3]

In other way forward information to your
accountant adviser.

EFTPS: The Electronic Federal Tax Payment
System PLEASE NOTE: Your tax payment is due
regardless of EFTPS online availability. In
case of an emergency, you can always make your
tax payment by calling the EFTPS.
```

ADVICE:

Never click on links in emails requesting personal information or to solve an urgent problem with an account. Simply open a new browser window and *manually* type in the web address of the bank or company (for example, manually type in: http://www.yourbank.com/). You can access your account or their customer service from there.

Here is one where they hope the victim will say to themselves, "hey, I didn't book that ticket, let me click on the link and see what this is about!"

EXAMPLE EMAIL:

```
From: "Qatar Airways"

Subject: Booking confirmation email

Thanks for the purchase!

Your booking is confirmed.

Booking number: K4QCTI

Your credit card has been charged for $438.60
(USD)

Please print the itinerary/receipt for your
reference.

Sign in to qatarairways.com and print it by
clicking the link below
```

```
[ed. different scammer web address linked on
this address]

https://booking.qatarairways.com/global/en/Get
PNRsListServle/

To cancel your booking online, please click
the link below:

[ed. different scammer web address linked on
this address]

https://booking.qatarairways.com/global/en/Can
celBookTripPlanServlet/

On board you will be offered:

- Beverages;

- Food;

- Daily press.

Thank you for choosing Qatar Airways and we
look forward to welcoming you on board.

Best regards,

Qatar Airways
```

And here is another banking example where the scammer's formatting job was not the greatest. Notice in the email headers the line that begins with 'Received:' - the actual source of the email is from India. It is sent in HTML so that when you click on the link to see why your password was changed, you do not see the actual web address you are going to (unless you mouse over it without clicking on it), which is a fake page where your password and other critical account information will be collected and stolen. They don't really care what the

REPLY-TO address is in this case, because they just want you to click on their hidden link and go to their bogus page that looks just like a Bank of America page.

EXAMPLE EMAIL:

```
Return-path:
[onlinebanking@ealerts.bankofamerica.com]

Received: from [122.175.140.46] (port=1768
helo=ABTS-MP-Dynamic-
046.140.175.122.airtelbroadband.in)
(envelope-from
<onlinebanking@ealerts.bankofamerica.com>)
From: "Bank of America Alert"
[onlinebanking@ealerts.bankofamerica.com]

To: [user email]

Cc: [user email]

Subject: Bank of America Alert: Email Address
Updated (sent to OLD email address)

Reply-To: "Bank of America Alert" <reply-
fefb7067070c99-91_HTML-626838614-99383-
6175695@ealerts.bankofamerica.com>

Bank of America

To ensure delivery, add
onlinebanking@ealerts.bankofamerica.com to
your address book.
Exclusively for:  |  [ed. user email inserted
here]

Online Banking Alert
Email

Address Updated
Security Checkpoint:
```

You last signed in to Online Banking on [ed. today's date inserted here].

Remember: Always look for your SiteKey(R) before entering your Passcode.
Your primary email address was set up or changed on [ed. today's date inserted here].

Your security is important to us. If you did not authorize this change, please contact us immediately at

Click Here [ed. scammer's redirected web address linked on the words 'Click Here'].

This Alert relates to your Online Banking profile, rather than a particular account. The account listed here is for verification purposes only.

Want to confirm this email is from Bank of America? Sign in to Online Banking and go to Alerts.

The Alerts History lists the Alerts sent to you in the past 60 days.

Like to get more Alerts? Sign in to your Online Banking account at Bank of America and within the Accounts Overview page select the Alerts tab.

Security Checkpoint:

This email includes a Security Checkpoint. The information in this section lets you know this is an authentic communication from Bank of America. Remember to look for your SiteKey every time you sign in to Online Banking.

Email Preferences

This is a service email from Bank of America. Please note that you may receive service email in accordance with your Bank of America

```
service agreements, whether or not you elect
to receive promotional email.

Contact us about this email

Please do not reply to this email with
sensitive information, such as an account
number, PIN, password, or Online ID. The
security and confidentiality of your personal
information is important to us. If you have
any questions, please either call the phone
number on your account statement or use the
Contact Us page, so we can properly verify
your identity.

Privacy and Security

Keeping your financial information secure is
one of our most important responsibilities.
For an explanation of how we manage customer
information, please read our Privacy Policy.
You can    also learn how Bank of America
keeps your personal information secure and how
you can help protect yourself.

Bank of America Email, 8th Floor-NC1-002-08-
25, 101 South Tryon St., Charlotte, NC 28255-
0001

Bank of America, N.A. Member FDIC. Equal
Housing Lender| 2012 Bank of America
Corporation.

All rights reserved.This email was sent to:
[ed. user email inserted here]

AR72768/DD6A66
```

Here is another example of an email where the scammers are hoping that you do not remember whether or not you had ever communicated with these people (notice how generic their email message is). Not being certain, you'll click on the link to see what it is about and get redirected to a site that either will be a sales pitch for their Viagra product, download a virus, or will ask you to login and provide your sensitive information.

EXAMPLE EMAIL:

Authentication-Results: sender-id=temperror (sender IP is 202.142.223.132) header.from=noreply@message.bsdeschacht.nl; dkim=none header.d=message.bsdeschacht.nl; x-hmca=none

X-SID-PRA: noreply@message.bsdeschacht.nl

Received: from mail.ascendits.net ([202.142.223.132]) by SNT0-MC4-F20.Snt0.hotmail.com with Microsoft SMTPSVC(6.0.3790.4900);

From: "Support Center" <noreply@message.bsdeschacht.nl>

Subject: Ticket [#25821780]

Return-Path: ticket@bsdeschacht.nl

Thank you for considering our products and services, your information arrived today.

Alright, here's the link to the site

http://newpillxdiet.com/

Thank you for taking the time to contact us.

Sincerely, Jaidyn Chambers, Support Team manager.

Disaster Relief Scams

Major disasters and traumatic events on a large human scale, things like 9-11 or the Japan tsunami or the Haiti earthquake disaster, bring out compassion in people and a need to want to contribute to healing and recovery. Charities fill this need and scammers have stepped in to create fake online charities. They create their websites on the heels of a major event and ask for donations and disappear with the money. Only give to well-known charities and make sure you are really at their legitimate website, or better yet – call them on the phone. Do not volunteer your bank account or credit card information online.

5. Fake Buyer Scam

This is the type of scam I typically deal with on my StopArtScams blog and Facebook page. It remains a very successful scam but I'm trying to change that. It is a scam where the perpetrator appears to be a legitimate purchaser. What you sell does not matter to them. They target anyone selling anything. Sometimes they try and construct their email to be very specific to the seller and other times the scammer will use a more generic email first, wait until people reply, and then fashion their more detailed "story". They are not after your stuff. They give out fake shipping addresses or more commonly refer to their shipping company helping them move who will come pick everything up – a shipping company that doesn't exist. So they don't care what you sell or where it goes. They are after your cash.

How It Works:

The scammer pretends to order an item (or a bunch of items) from you. They offer to pay by certified check or credit card. If you agree, they ask for your address so they can mail the check (or provide you the credit card number). They crank up the urgency in their story and tell you they will be using their shipper because they are moving a lot of items to their new home and the shippers will come by and get the items they've purchased from you. They send you the check, sometimes overnight, or push you to process the credit card quickly. If you accepted the check, when you receive it you will see it is for more than the amount of the order, often by $1000-$5000 or more. They continue their story and tell you to deposit the money and forward the difference on to the shipper who needs to be paid as well. Oh, and of course, there is some reason why the shipper can't accept payment any other way than Western Union wire transfer.

If you fell all the way through this scam, you would soon discover their money is fake (the check is fraudulent and the bank will find that out soon enough; or the credit card number is stolen and often not yet reported so it might actually clear but will always result in a charge back). In the meantime, you have forwarded your good money to a shipper who doesn't exist (or there is a shipping company with that name but they have no business relationship with the scammer), via Western Union. Once the scammer picks up the money at the other end, it is untraceable and they have vanished with your money.

This whole scheme would go away if Western Union, and other wire transfer services, would not be such a haven for untraceable transactions. Scammers can even look up online at Western Union if their money from the victim has come in—at least at MoneyGram (which also is a haven for untraceable money transactions) they have to physically go to the MoneyGram office to check.

Scam Alert Flags

- the perpetrator has some story about moving to a foreign country or being "at sea"

- often the perpetrator is ordering too much or has no idea what they are ordering

- the perpetrator insists on using their third-party shipping company

– the perpetrator eventually asks that money be forwarded via Western Union

– the perpetrator says they like your items and want to order a quantity but then asks for your website address

– the email has the usual spelling, grammar and formatting errors

– they make up fake names and sometimes spell their own fake names incorrectly

TIP: Never forward money to third-party strangers online. Do a search online for name, email address, store name, shipping company BEFORE sending any items or money.

Variations:

I've seen this same scam used to also target music, art, and dance teachers giving lessons. Instead of a shipping company, they order lessons and overpay (by "mistake") and ask that the overpayment be sent back to them via Western Union. You deposit their fake money and forward the overpayment from your real money and then they disappear. Here is an example for the services of a massage therapist

EXAMPLE EMAIL:

From:Roberto bocca
[mailto:therapiabocca@suomi24.fi]

Subject: Enquiry for a Massage Therapist

Greetings from Milan,

My name is Roberto bocca, I live and work as a massage therapist here in Italy . I am 46 yrs old. I have been doing massage since 1991. I do a deep relaxation massage in which the muscles relax without pain. I also do energy massage that helps people feel great when I am done. I am also certified to do pregnancy massage. I have lots of happy clients here in italy .

I have been looking for a massage therapist for over a week now till i met an old friend yesterday that referred you to me, her name is Serah. She used to live in America before she relocated here with her family, so i decided to contact you to know if you will be able to give my client some massage sessions when she arrives the US.

My clients name is Ms Alice Raffael, she is a model here in Italy. She will be coming to the U.S in 2 weeks time for a modeling job and will be residing in California temporarily until the neccesary arrangement for her job has been made before she leaves. She will be needing 1hr massage session per day, 2 Sessions per week for 6 weeks when she arrives.

Ms Raffael asked me to come with her to the US but i told her i would not be able to go with her to the US as i have a course i will be going for in a week time, so i promised to help her find a good massage therapist in your Area.

Pls tell me a little more about your self, how long have you been a massage therapist? Would you be able to provide her with the massage sessions from the 14th of next month to the 22nd of December, 2 Sessions per week for 6 weeks?

Pls i need you to get back to me with the amount you charge per session and also let me know if she can pay you with a Certified check drawn from a US bank?

Do send your reply to my personal email address { roberto.bocca@yahoo.it } for a quick response as i do not check this email always.

Till I read from you remain blessed.

Roberto bocca

622 Via Mercato,

1,56129

Milano Italy

This same scam—overpaying for an item with fraudulent money, is highly prevalent on sites like Craigslist as well.

ADVICE:

NEVER do a business transaction involving Western Union. Sorry, Western Union, but it's true. Same with MoneyGram. Never do a business transaction where you are forwarding money from an overpayment to some other party. In fact, don't accept overpayments. And for most people, never agree to use the buyer's third-party shipper. Use your own.

What will happen when you insist on any of these requirements? The scammer will quickly disappear and move on to focus on other victims.

Here is an example of a more generic approach to this scam.

EXAMPLE EMAIL:

```
From: cody morgan [codymorgan2010@gmail.com]

Subject: General Inquiry

Dear Sales, Good day to you, Am Cody Morgan by
name, kindly answer the following question: 1:
Can you ship to Atlanta, GA 30310 . Do you
Accept Pick Up? 2: Do you accept Credit Cards
account details for only form of payment your
swift response will be highly appreciated.
Best regards Cody Morgan DIANE INC 734 DAYNA
DR, , ATLANTA, GA 30349
```

And another generic email example.

EXAMPLE EMAIL:

```
From: Ladd Smith [smithladd@yahoo.com]

Subject: ORDER

Hello there,

I will like to place an order for art piece to
my location in Malaysia, kindly let me know if
you can charge directly on my credit card(U.S.
funds) for payment.

I have a shipper who can also get the order to
my doorstep in Malaysia.

Await your timely reply.

Thank you.

Ladd
```

Here is an example email where they started generically and are now speaking more specifically because the user responded to their first email.

EXAMPLE EMAIL:

```
----- Forwarded Message -----

From: "Elaine Jackson"
[eljackson.05@gmail.com]

Subject: Payment Delivered:Get the ball
rolling

Hi Rick,
```

Thanks so much for your prompt response to my email this morning,and I'm grateful to you that you understand what I`m going through at the moment.I checked the fedex website just now and found that the payment for those creative works I am purchasing from you has been delivered at exactly 10:30 AM,the check is a refund for a canceled order as a result of our recent relocation plan.

Therefore,I will like you to proceed to your bank to deposit the check as soon as the funds has been processed by your bank we can proceed with the shipments. The rest of the funds will be for the shipment of the artworks and the other house items we are moving to our new home in Johannesburg. You will do me a favor to pay the movers when they come for the pick up.The Shipper had advised us that he will forward the information you need for the remittance as soon as they can.

I will look forward to hearing from you as soon as you have deposited the check so that I can contact the person that issued the payment to facilitate its prompt clearance at your bank.

Regards,

Elaine

And here is a later response from a scammer that is much more specific but still has the convoluted story about payment, to get you to forward money to a third party.

EXAMPLE EMAIL:

From: Andrew Roundy
[mailto:roundyandrew1@gmail.com]

Subject: ITEMS NEEDED........CONTACT SHIPPER

Hello

Good to read back from you . below are the Items I want to order,

Sea Salt Grinder $5.29

60 qty

Organic BBQ- $6.29

60 qty

Mixed Herb- $6.29

60 qty

Vegetable- $6.29

60 qty

SHIPPING ADDRESS

16 Ayala Avenue,

Makati City,

Metro Manila, Philippines 1226

Concerning the shipment,the likes of UPS,FEDEX and POST OFFICE always don't take care of the charges down here. Charges like handling, customs duties,tax etc. I have experienced such situation before and I don't want to be the victims of such a thing again. I will be glad if you contact this freight forwarder Seahog Logistics Ltd for shipping quote.The shipping company will arrange the pick-up of my order from your store,so you don't have any stress to face in shipping processing at all.Here is their email address (seahoglogistics@yahoo.com) ,Not that I can't deal with the shipper directly,but they always prefer to deal with the store where they will be doing the pick up in other to reduce the customs duties and other charges.They have a way of preparing their shipment documents whereby the custom duties payment on this goods will be reduced and if I wanted to pay for the custom duties and other charges, at times it is 40% of the whole package amount.I do trust Seahog Logistics Ltd ,if not I wouldn't have recommend them for my shipment.They are very reliable and fast.They will take care of everything including Handling, Customs duties,Tax, Insurance etc.Contact them to obtain a quote and get back to me in the format bellow:

COST OF THE ORDER

COST OF THE SHIPPING FROM SEAHOG LOGISTICS LTD

TOTAL COST (ORDER + SHIPPING)

Once I have these details from you, I will get back to you with my credit card information,so you can charge and make the necessary shipping arrangements.

Regards,

Andrew

NOTE:The freight company will need these 5 information to get you a quote,so provide them with the details bellow:

1)My Customer's ID # :AQW364626YA

2)Delivery Full Address:

16 Ayala Avenue,

Makati City,

Metro Manila, Philippines 1226.

3)Pick Up Full Address : PROVIDE YOUR ADDRESS

4)Weight Of The Consignment : PROVIDE ORDER WEIGHT

5)Momentary Value Of The Consignment : PROVIDE ORDER TOTAL COST

And of course here is an example of a scammer targeting artists, which is what got me all riled up to begin with (these scammers will find names of the artwork pieces either on the artist's website or a more collective spot, like eBay).

EXAMPLE EMAIL:

From: Anita Primoff [animoffty@gmail.com]

Subject: Artworks purchase

Good day to you.

I am so excited that I came across of your work on internet search,I am interested in purchasing these creative artworks from you....................

Yellowstone:Meadow Light Morning,Spring Edge

plein aire oil paintings:2,5 & 11

Let me know their various prices.and how much discounts are you going to give?I will be happy to have these selected artworks hung in our new home in South Africa.As well,I want you to take out the shipping cost.I have been in touch with a shipping firm that will be shipping other house decoratives.

We are traveling from our Seattle home to our new apartment as soon as possible.On Paying for the artworks,I will be glad to pay you with a Money Order or Cashier`s check in US funds that can be easily cashed at your local bank,please let me know on how to proceed for the payment of the creative artworks.

I will await your advise on how to proceed.Have a wonderful day.

Take care,

Anita Primoff

In this example, you can see how the scammer wants to rush the victim through the scam before they've had time to consider the appropriateness of what they are doing.

Also, this particular scammer included the "cash the check" scam strategy in here as well—offering to pay $50 incentive for cashing the check (also notice how he is rushing to pay for something he hasn't even seen pictures of yet).

EXAMPLE EMAIL:

FROM: James Mack [jamesmack35@aol.com]

Good, the price is fine and I will buy from you but the issue is

I have a tight schedule planning for my wedding so the following

details is needed for mailing and issueing you

a money order,

....

full Name ____?

address____?

City_____?

state ________?

Zip Code_____?

phone #_________?

Info is required so I mail you the payment asap via Usps courier service and pick up will be done by a shipper at my cost after you've cashed the check,I'll also include an extra $50 for your run around while cashing it.Hope you reply soon,my details is as follows............

james mack

10100 Silver Mountain Drive,

Austin, TX , 78737

NOTE: If available I'll appreciate some pictures along with the details.

THANKS.

james mack

You can see many additional examples of actual emails of this type of scam at http://stopartscams.blogspot.com

6. Online Jobs Scam

So many people are out of work and looking for ways to make money in order to pay bills. This scam has been around for a long time but in these tough economic conditions, it has found a growing number of victims.

How It Works:

Scammers will both post job openings and also reach out to job seekers who have posted their resume, with at least some personal data accessible by potential employers, on legitimate employment sites. The job offer might be to become become a "financial representative" of a company overseas you have never heard of before. They will explain the reason they are hiring is that their company has problems accepting money from US customers and they need assistance in handling those payments. They might offer to pay you 5 to 15 percent commission per transaction.

When you apply for the job, you might be asked to provide the scammer with your personal data, like your bank account information, so you can "get paid". Instead of ever being paid, the scammer is likely to proceed with the following:

– steal your identity,

– steal money from your bank account,

– ask you to deposit checks they send you, keep a percentage for yourself, and send the rest back to the employer.

Another version of this same scam involves products. It is sometimes referred to as the "Re-Ship Scam".

In this scam, criminals post job announcements on legitimate Internet career sites offering work-at-home positions—sometimes advertised as "merchandising manager" or "package processing assistant." Job responsibilities will typically include receiving packages and then mailing them to foreign addresses, using postage-paid mailing labels provided via email.

If you accept the job, the packages you receive will typically contain:

– Merchandise purchased with stolen credit cards, and/or

– Counterfeit postal money orders, which the scammer will ask you to send to other scammers, unbeknownst to you.

And when you receive payment, the check or postal money order you receive will turn out to be all counterfeits. Sometimes, the scammers will work with a victim up to the point where they are suppose to now pay the victim, usually about month after starting the job.

They will drop them and disappear about a day or so before the victim begins to expect to be paid for their work.

An example of another bogus work-at-home job is the paid "mystery shoppers".

If you sign up for the job, the scammer will send you money for your mystery shopping, while instructing you to keep your earned portion and forward the remainder of the amount elsewhere via wire transfer. Sound familiar? The check they send will turn out to be fraudulent and you've forwarded on your good money and so end up not being paid and out the money amount you forwarded, typically just back to them at the other end of that wire transfer.

ADVICE:

Check to make sure a money order is legitimate BEFORE you deposit it. Once a bank identifies a deposited check as fraudulent, they take the money back out of your account and hold you responsible for that amount. To verify if a postal money order is authentic, call the USPS Postal Inspector's Money Order Verification System at 1-866-459-7822.

EXAMPLE EMAIL:

Hello! We noted your interest in our Purchasing Manager/Agent vacancy, which we opened last week. It is my pleasure to write to you with a description of the position and company. The description of the position itself is attached as Job Description file. You will find more about the base wage, working schedule and hours, base commissions and benefits, location and the closing date for the position, about mission and the culture of our organization from that file. Full and Part time positions are opened. You are free to start as Part Time position and switch to Full Time later. This is work at home position (or anywhere you are) . There is NO relocation required. There is NO fee to apply.

Apart from that file, I send you company's Application Form. If you are interested, please complete the Application Form and return it to current email or by fax number listed below:

1) by mail: you may simply download the Application Form, complete the Application Form by required information and send it back to my email.

2) by Fax: you may simply download the Application Form, print it and complete by required information to send back at fax number listed below.

After short consideration, we will arrange an interview. Further details regarding the interview process will be sent to successful candidates. Appropriate training will be provided for successful candidates.

If you have any further queries please do not hesitate to contact me on my office extension. My telephone and fax numbers are as below. I am directing my personal attention to this matter.

Best Regards,

HR Manager Linda Williams

Phone: (646)257-xxxx

Fax: (718)819-xxxx

In this example, the scammer sent out this email to people, whether or not they had applied for any job. They are hoping to catch some victims who receive this email and just happen to be job hunting and don't remember all the places they've applied. So they will click on the link to see what it is about.

EXAMPLE EMAIL:

From: Diana Hester (brandi@ssintl.org)

Subject: Your Job Application - Action Required

Hello

Thank you for submitting your information for potential employment opportunities.

We look forward to reviewing your application, but can not do so until you complete our internal application.

Prior to begin able to be considered, you will first need you to formally apply.

Please go here to begin the process:

http://rzxmanagement.ru
Also, the following perks are potentially available:
- Paid Time Off
- Health Benefits Package
- Higher than average salaries
- Tuition Reimbursement
- Extensive 401(k)program

Please take the time to follow the directions and complete the entire application process.

This example email was sent and made to appear it came from a company posting on the CareerBuilder website.

EXAMPLE EMAIL:

Our new position: You can start tomorrow

Unfortunately, I wasn't able to reach you via phone today. Therefore, I would like to follow-up my voicemail with an email.

The reason for this email is that our company is looking to hire. Please see below for more information on the role.

Job Description :

Checking emails daily

You can keep the actual job

US citizen or permanent residence/green card holder

Honesty, responsibility and promptness in operations

Self-motivated and capable of working

```
independently

Required Travel: NO

NO SALES

21 years +

What we offer:

Our team members also enjoy a comprehensive
benefits program including:

· 1,800$ fixed salary + commission + Bonus for
each transaction you will take the money
upfront.

· $85,000 - $95,000 per year

· Opportunities for career advancement.

If you're interested in our opportunities or
want more information about our program,
please please reply here. If you're not
interested, maybe you have a friend or
colleague who can benefit from our great
opportunities.

I look forward to helping you find your next
position!

Best regards,

Human Resources
```

Scam Alert Flags

- the web address in the email link does not exactly match the company's web address (mouse over the link without clicking on it)

– communications which ask you to reply to a private email outside the company's email address

– flagrant misspellings and grammar mistakes throughout email

– asking for personal and sensitive information in very first email

TIPS:

– whether or not a prospective employer claims to be doing a 'routine background check', under no circumstances should you give them your Social Security number

– prospective employers also would never need your bank account number or even credit card number

– you may think you are dealing with a real employer who has asked you to fax a form with all your private information, but double-check the fax number to verify it is a legitimate company fax destination

7. Stranded Scam

This may happen to you or, more likely, you will get one of these emails from someone you know who has you on their email contact list.

How It Works:

The hackers get access to your Yahoo, Hotmail or Gmail account. How do they get access? They've either tricked you into clicking on a link and providing them the password (see "Phishing Scams") OR some scammers just get access by using software that is constantly trying combinations of passwords and it alerts them when they've hit a correct combination and can then get into your account.

Once they have access, the scammer sends out an email (see the example that follows) to everyone in the contact address book of the account they've just hacked into. The tricky part of this scam is the email is actually coming from the hacked account so it does appear to be coming from someone you are familiar with. This is the part that makes this scam so successful.

In the following email example, you'll notice the goal of the scam is to get the receiver of the email to reply and send money. But here is how you'll recognize this as a scam: the 'Reply-To' email looks almost identical to the victim's account they've hacked but it IS different. The 'Reply-To' email is where a response from you will go, and the scammer wants to receive your reply so the 'Reply-To' will be different than the 'From' email address. In many cases the 'Reply-To' address is just one letter or number different from the real thing. This will be unnoticeable to the reader who is not looking carefully at the headers of the email.

EXAMPLE EMAIL:

```
Subject: Worst Case!!! (Need help)

I'm am in a deep mess right now and i need
your help.I am in tears as i am writing you
now,sorry I didn't inform you about my trip,I
had a trip to the United
Kingdom(Buckinghamshire) and a bizarre thing
happened to me.I was mugged at gun point last
night, it happened at the park of the Hotel
were i lodged but thank God i wasn't hurt, the
muggers carted away with all my belongings
excluded my passport. Cell,c-card,cash and
some important documents are all gone.I was
able to make contact with the Uk Police and i
was directed to the Embassy, but they seems to
be taking things too slow.

I need your help so urgently.. My flight
leaves pretty soon but i am having problems
sorting out the hotel bills and also need
getting my ticket straightened out. I need
your help. I need a quick loan from you to get
things fixed out here, promise to refund as
soon as i get back home. Your support and
assistance will go a long way here.please
reply asap so i can tell you what to do and
how to get the money to me via western
union..Hope to read from you soon.

Sherry
```

What to do if you've been hacked like this? Change your password immediately (and make it harder to guess) and then send out an email to everyone in your address book. Put in the subject line something to alert your people not to respond to the previous email. Not much more you can do. If it is someone you know who has been hacked, send them an email and let them know their account has been compromised and they need to change their password right away and alert the people on their contact list that their account was hacked and they are not, in fact, stranded and in need of money.

EXAMPLE EMAIL:

```
From: [ed. person's name and email that you
know]

Subject: Help Needed Asap!!! ([ed. name of
person you know inserted here])

Reply-To: [ed. person's same username as her
yahoo account but now at live.com]@live.com

To:

Hello,

I'm writing this with tears in my eye, I came
down to London, United Kingdom for a short
vacation and got mugged at the park of the
hotel where i stayed, all our cash, credit
card and cell were stolen off us at GUN POINT
but luckily for me i still have my passport
with me but don't have enough money to sort
the bills so i can get out of here.

I've been to the embassy and the cops but
they're not helping issues at all and my
flight leaves soon and the hotel manager won't
let me leave until i settle the bills, I'm
```

```
freaked out at the moment and wondering if you
could help me with a quick loan, I promise
I'll refund it once we get home. Please write
me so i can send you the info for the wire of
the money to save me from the embarrassment of
not being able to cover the bills. Am really
sorry for the odd request

Hope to read back from you soonest

[your friend's name here]
```

8. Counterfeit Postal Money Orders

Counterfeit postal money orders can be a scam in and of itself or be a component of many other types of scams, such as overpayment scams, job scams, mystery shopper scams, etc. These counterfeit money orders usually originate in foreign countries and can even sometimes be accompanied by a fake letter of authenticity by the USPS.

How It Works:

When a scammer replies to a classified ad, auction posting, or any selling site like Etsy or just a small business website, they will offer to pay for the item with a check, and then begin describing some made-up reason for writing the check for more than the purchase price, typically by $1000-$5000. The scammer will then ask the seller to wire back the difference after depositing the check. If the seller does deposit the check, the bank will often accept it and the seller might be lulled into thinking it must be good but the bank will eventually process it as fraudulent (it can take days but sometimes weeks) and the seller is left liable for the entire amount, yet the seller's good money has already been forwarded to the scammer via wire transfer. Once the scammer picks it up from a place like Western Union or MoneyGram, it is completely untraceable and the scammer and the seller's money gone, gone, gone.

When scammers set up a "job" for a secret, or mystery, shopper, the shopper asked to test the effectiveness of a money transfer service and what they really end up doing is being trapped in a counterfeit check cashing scam. As the scam goes, the shopper is sent a check, which is fake, and asked to deposit it in their bank account, withdraw a certain amount in cash and send that cash back to the employer via wire transfer – and then evaluate their experience of the service. But you see the problem. They are not evaluating anything and they just lost a bunch of their good money. This is a scam that works.

Scammers count on the confusion that might be created when a person deposits one of their counterfeit checks. The bank, by law, has to make that money available by the next business day. Now the user thinks it must be good because their funds are available. And that is what the scammer wants the user to believe. But banks have the right to later take that money back if the check is found to be fraudulent, which it will be, and the depositor is responsible for the full amount. By that time the victim has already forwarded cash to the scammer so they are out of luck.

And I'll say it again – do NOT accept overpayments and do not forward overpayments to anyone via wire transfer.

How to Recognize a Fake Money Order

1. Watermarks: Watermarks of Benjamin Franklin, seen both on the front and back when held up to light, can be found on official U.S. postal money orders. A counterfeit money order will either have these watermarks missing or altered.

2. Security Threads: There are security threads of official money orders that are actually embedded in the paper. The same security threads can be found in paper money. For postal money orders, look for a dark the security thread that runs from the top of the money order to the bottom, and to the right of watermark from the front view. You'll see USPS multiple times on the thread, especially when held up to the light.

3. Amount: Legitimate money orders are limited by how much money they can represent. Fake money orders sometimes have amounts higher than this. There is no

cash value to postal money orders that exceed $1000 in the United States and $700 for international money orders.

4. Color: Check for the green, yellow, blue color scheme on domestic postal money orders and pink, yellow, and gold on international.

5. Smudges and Alterations: Often counterfeit money orders will look like the unique ID number has been changed or the dollar amount has been altered.

Authorization Documents: Authorization Documents: In order to trick victims into believing their fake money order is actually a real money order, some scammers will include a fake letter that claims to come from the USPS (United States Postal Service) stating that the sender is authorized by the USPS to issue and negotiate postal money orders. Don't believe it. There is no such letter from the USPS, they just don't do this. Only scammers offer this letter.

TIP: To verify if a postal money order is authentic, call the Money Order Verification System at 1-866-459-7822.

9. Dating Scam

Scammers also create faked profiles on dating sites in order to prey upon vulnerable people. Sometimes referred as the "sweetheart swindle", this scam has been around a long, long time offline as well. Unfortunately, there always seems to be a ready pool of lonely hearts out there ready to be potential victims for this scam.

How It Works:

This is a scam that takes time and commitment on the part of the scammer, but they feel their payoff is worth the effort. They will respond to people's profiles on dating sites. Lately, many of them pretend to be in the military. They will have a made-up "backstory" about who they are and email with you over a period of weeks. They are checking to see how vulnerable and how likely you are to believe you are in love with someone you have never met and only know online. Once they have you all hooked in, they may ask for your help to reship packages Europe or Africa. Or they may make requests for money, which they'll position as "loans". Soon they are asking for a loan to borrow money so they can come see you. But that meeting is never going to happen and your money is gone.

A very similar variation is referred to as the "lonely

hearts" scam. Men, for example, will receive photos of an attractive woman looking for a husband. If they respond, the woman claims very quickly to be in love with them and asks for money to pay for an airline ticket so they can meet. If they send the money, the woman will come up with another reason to ask for yet more money. The woman's photos are fake and it very likely isn't even a woman. But this scam goes both ways. Women falls for non-existent men and men fall for non-existent women.

In another example, a woman was on Match.com and started corresponding with a man claiming to be in the military. His profile said he was 39 and the woman was 61 so she said he was too young. He wrote back and said he had made a mistake in his profile (yeah, right...), that he was actually in his late forties. So the woman said she believed him because he was in the military. She knew she wouldn't date him but they became pen pals and later she would say she felt love. Then he talks of coming to visit her and sends her papers to fill out for his release. Of course, these papers asked for all kinds of personal and financial information. That raised a flag for her and she began researching more, finding out that civilians can't request leaves in behalf of military people. He had also asked for $850 to process the paperwork. Scammers just love to go for as much as they can.

So she didn't lose her money or information, fortunately, but she still felt quite embarrassed and ashamed that she had let this scammer string her along for so long.

Another woman, newly separated from a 42 year marriage went on an online dating site and began corresponding with a man who claimed to be a 55 year old widow, that his wife had died twelve years ago, his profile said he was half English and half Hungarian, that he'd lived in America for a long time but he now had houses in Virginia, the U.S. and Croydon, and that he worked as a self-employed petroleum engineer earning 100,000 a year traveling around the world.

They corresponded for weeks and then he began the scam. It started by him calling from an airport on his way to a conference (all made up) and asking if she could top off his cell phone balance. He corresponded for more weeks and then a friend called saying he had gotten in an accident and a few days later he called asking for a "loan" for his hospital bills. He then said because he was out of commission, he needed help bridging a contract to buy equipment and he would give her a percentage of the contract for helping him keep it alive. Several weeks later he was diagnosed with prostrate cancer and she sent more money. By the time he began making arrangements to fly and see her – asking her for the money to do that, the woman's daughter became aware of what was going on and stopped it, but not before this woman basically had lost her life savings in the scam.

Once a scammer knows they have someone who is willing to send money, they will just keep going and going until they get every last penny they can.

Scam Alert Flags

– you receive "I love you" messages almost immediately

– the person is asking for money or a loan, or to cash a check or money order for them

– they claim to b a wealthy person who is abroad a lot

– they may ask you to help them out with a business deal

– they suddenly need help paying for medical expenses for a parent or child's operation, or sometimes their own operation

– the person's photo on the dating site will seem very attractive but they are unwilling to send any other photos

TIPS FOR AVOIDING THIS SCAM:

– establish an anonymous email account from an email service. Change your account information so it does not give out your full name. This will protect your privacy more as it's pretty easy to get information on a person from an email address that you've used for years.

– if you don't want your home address to be known, use your cell phone number, if you don't have that listed online in association with your home address. Use an unlisted number, if possible. Do not let them call you with a 'caller unknown" caller ID.

– most of these scams work because the scammer is located in another country. They are not local but eventually start asking for flight money to come meet you. You'll do better if you just decide from the onset that you are not going to give anyone money that you are about to date, thinking of dating, newly dating – maybe never.

EXAMPLE EMAIL:

Hi Ben. Have good day? I waited your letter and was very much Is pleased, when you have written to me. I am waiting for your letters every day! Your physik was interesting to me Is pleased, that we begin to learn each other more well and to develop Our acquaintance. I think, that it is an interesting thing, to learn someone far through the Internet. It is unusual to me, because I a little Is familiar with the Internet.

Ben, I want to inform you, that I have no the computer at home also I go in Internet - cafe, in free from work time. That To translate my letters to you I use the electronic program The interpreter, because for me is faster and it is convenient to write for you In Russian, and then to translate the letter on English. I hope, That you can understand well my letters. I studied the English language Earlier at school, and after that in college and I understand your letters very well. Only please do not use Reductions of words. While I did not establish the computer in the house, therefore That I have no there telephone. It would be interesting to me to speak with you and If you not against, I could in the future try To cause you, that we could speak about different things. Ben, I want To tell to you it is a little about itself. I live in city Obst and I have very good family. Because of my work I take off a small apartment and I live in it separately from my family. But I very much frequently reach to them and I spend with them weekend. we frequently we are chosen together on a camping and We have other entertainments. Mine the city not of the large size, and in it is a little The people. Basically at us in city various factory and factories. Is present Some restaurant and bar. The city is constructed not by high houses till 3-5 floors. About 20 kilometers from it there is a very large and modern city Minsk. I with the friends frequently get out there to buy some Things or fashionable clothes. I work, my job that I create various holidays, concert programs. now I work as the senior seller in shop, which sells female footwear. I have in my submission 3 men.

My work brings to me not so many money, but it is pleasant to me. And also I work as the seller in this shop. Tell to me about the job. She is pleasant to you? To me my job is pleasant. I very much like to laugh and I respect the people with good By humour. I like to travel. I yet was not far from mine At home, but I dream in the future to visit in different places. I 2-3 times in Week go to be engaged in sports hall, to hold my body in The order. And you Ben, have any sports in the life? You love Entertainment on a nature? A hunt? fishing? A camping? Some inform me Things about the entertainment. It will be very interesting to me to learn about it. I wait for your letters.

Sincerely yours Elena.

Me mail Elen6524@MAIL.RU

And here is a typical letter once they've exchanged a few emails, have already "fallen in love", and "she" wants to meet.

EXAMPLE EMAIL:

Hello my love Dave. I am again happy to see your letter. All necessary documents and services of the company will cost 450 dollars and 750 air tickets. In general I need 1200 dollars. Lovely, you can find out this information it is direct from visa agency www.visas.ru they work with the American embassy since 1991 and well know all "reefs" of process of registration of visas in this embassy. Lovely, I am very sad, when I have found out cost of the visa. I simply can not pay it. For me it is impossible, as I earn the salary 140 dollars per one month. It's make me little suppressed and disappointed. I don't have so much now. I was make application but I must pay for it. I asked my mother about our savings she said that the money should not be a barrier between two people which love each other. I counted my sum and I found out that I have only about fifty dollars and my wages. will be not soon. I asked my friends about helping me and they said that have not at the present moment. I asked the advice my mother and she said that maybe you can help me, because you loves me. I asked her how he can help me, because he is far from me. My mother said that you can send the money through company which make this service. I asked about it, on my work and I know now, that exists reliable and fast company, which makes remittances in world and it's western union. I remember that I saw advertising this company on tv. I take a directory book and found the address of it and it's not far from me. I went there, and I asked them about service. They said that sender must go to the western union, give them information: the name and last name of receiver, country they make transfer and bring the ten digits secret code to sender. The receiver must know ten digits for receiving money. They say that the branches of it must be everywhere worldwide.

Here is the information about me:

Country: Russia

City: Omsk

Name: Aleksandra

Lastname: Liholetova

Address of branch of western union:

ALFA BANK

zipcode: 644001,

Omsk,

Street. Kuibyshev, 79

The phone: 3812 53-51-76

I must know your full name, full address and 10 figures (MTCN) You must know that I decide to ask you about it because I love you and trust you very much. I decide to come to you because I feel this way and you are very necessary to me, decided to come to the unfamiliar country and I never be outside my country. But I decided to do it because now you are part of my life and I trust you in all. My love I need 1200 american dollars I think you will help me because we found our love and we want to meet closer. You must inform me ten digits and I can receive it. You must know we must hurry because I can receive the documents soon, and if we lost the time it is necessary for a long time. Now it's very difficultly to receive the visa to your country, and it's fact, but if I pay now, I think I do it. I think about sense of money, and I'm very sad if this paper can prevent people to meet each other. In most cases the money play a main role in life but it's not right! I'm sure. And the quantity of money was and will not important to me, I always not aspired to material enrichment and don't search specially for rich male. I appreciate human qualities and relations, and I love you Dave!!! I love you all my heart, I want to be with you now. I want to be with you forever. If it's mutually we will be very happy in our life. I think you love me too and we will meet very soon. You are my love, my Angel. My heart is yours. I'm waiting good news from you, I hope everything will be all right and we will be together soon. Every day I think about our meeting, and I think it's real, we must use this chance of destiny.

I LOVE YOU!!!!!!!!

Always your love Aleksandra.

10. Identity Theft

Identity theft is a crime in which a person uses the identity of someone they are not, typically for financial gain. In today's high-tech fast-moving automated society, you are often asked to provide pieces of information about yourself, such as social security numbers, a signature, name, address, phone numbers, and even banking and credit card information in some cases. The scammers love that the Internet makes this so easy for them. If a scammer is able to access your personal information, he or she can use it to commit fraud in your name. With identity theft, criminals do things such as apply for loans or new credit card accounts. They will then request a billing address change, you won't see your bill while they run up charges on it without your knowledge. They'll keep going if they can. They'll use counterfeit checks and open debit cards, and even authorize electronic transfers in your name to wipe out your bank account. They can do a lot of damage before they are even noticed and it can sometimes take years to clear the bad reports on your record.

Advanced identity thieves will take this activity beyond even monetary gains – they will use your information to obtain a driver's license or other documentation that would display their photo but your name and information. They will use these documents to obtain a job and file fraudulent income tax returns, or apply for travel documents, file insurance claims. They even can provide your name and mailing address to police and if caught in a crime.

This scam activity is less about trying to get money out of you and more about trying to get your personal information. It may be done by "phishing" (sending an email that looks like it is coming from your bank and asking you to log in from a link in the email when, in fact, it is a fake site the scammer has set up) or even posting fake job ads. In our examples that follow, the scammers posted fake job ads on Craigslist.

EXAMPLE EMAIL:

From : Fred Thomas

Subject : RE: Part time Admin. Assistant Position

Hello Applicant,

Hope you're having a pleasant day today? You contacted me applying for the position which I advertised on Craigslist. Do take time to go through this introductory mail and feel free to pass any questions on.

Fred Thomas is My name.I have been a Fashion Designer for over 30 years and i have been teaching too and i also has been running a fabrics company for 20 years. I bring a unique teaching style to students which will guarantee creative and fun learning by all student fashion designers while elevating them to new, exciting designers heights that they have only dreamed of.I often conduct LIVE slide/talk lectures on Understanding Exposure, the Art of Seeing, throughout the USA, Great Britain and Asia.At the moment, I am in a work-ship in the England.I will be here for a month after which I will fly down to Philippines for a Live-slide/talk show lectures with some students.

YOUR DUTIES AS MY PERSONAL ASSISTANT.

While I am out of the United State,I need some one who can stand in the gap for me.His/her duties will be the following

1.To receive letters and mails on my behalf.

2.Receive cheques and money orders from clients who want to attend the forth coming workshops or Live shows.

3.Schedule appointments for me.

4.Book my flight tickets.

5.Send letters and mails from my clients.

This position is home-based and flexible part time job,you can be in any location to carry out any of the activities.All you need do is to check your emails twice daily and keep your phone on most times in case i might need to call you from anywhere i may be.I do have a number of things you could help me with this week if you will be available to start.This can act as a stable foundation to our working relationship.Let me know if you have any of the office equipment (If not,I will make arrangements to send them to your address

Printer:

Personal Laptop/Desktop:

Internet Access:

Scanner:

Fax machine:

Laminator:

Paper Cutter:

For proper review(since i am not available now to set up a face-to-face interview) supply out correctly the information below .

FIRST NAME ....LAST NAME...................

ADDRESS.................

CITY ....STATE.......................

ZIP CODE............COUNTRY.................

PHONE NUMBER (S) ....

PRESENT OCCUPATION..............................

GENDER.............MARITAL STATUS........

AGE.............NATIONALITY...........

Email...................

Scanned copy of your ID:(You can provide that later when you are employed)

Note: It will be of added advantage if you can provide 2 references from your past employments.

Qualification:

1.Educational background is not a criteria.

2.You must be Organized and able to take instructions well Dependable, Reliable, Trustworthy a must

3.Must have excellent English language skills (both spoken and written)

4.Have great work ethic and attitude, as well as people skills, pay-attention to detail, capable of multi-tasking, and works well under stress at times.

Benefits:

- Yearly performance bonus

- Paid vacation/sick/personal days

- Medical benefits

Salary:

500 USD weekly(2,000USD monthly)

Also,there will be compensation for efficiency and hard working.

Thanks

Fred Thomas.

EXAMPLE EMAIL:

Thank you for applying for the Marketing Manager position with Arthur Galagher. I just had a chance to review your resume and am going to send your application through for hiring. If you are not interested in the job please let me know no later than Wednesday so I can look at other candidates.

The position will start in 3 weeks, and pay is negotiable so you will need to start thinking about your salary requirements so we can discuss them later this week. I would like to give you a call, what's the best time to reach you and at what number? You can email me at my personal account, which is arthurgalagherhrdir@safe-mail.net. My office line is 1-310-388-5791.

The position will require a background check because of the nature of the high level of security that we have with several of our clients. I am attaching the form in this email. Just open it up, fill it out, and fax it back to 1-775-923-7229, that's a secured fax line to the company that handles all the screening. They usually take a few days to get them done, so if you could get it done by Wednesday I would appreciate it. Email me when you're through, and we can go from there.The payment code, which goes on, the application is: 2545-2251-3629-8907. If you don't put that on there they wont process it, or maybe they will get in touch with you and try to get you to pay for the screening, so make sure you don't forget to put the payment info on there so they can bill us for it.

I will need to also set up an in person interview with you, and would like to get it done by Friday. Are there any days that don't/ won't work for you? If there are any problems email them to me, and either me or my assistant, Hanna Andrews will get back with you.I look forward to meeting you and I will talk to you early next week.

Sincerely,William T. Levinski

Human Resources Director

Arthur Galagher Insurance

PS. I am going to set up an account for you on our secure server so you can access our site and projects. Email me a four digit (have to be numbers no letters) so I can set it as your pass code. Your username will be your first

```
middle and last name. You can change it once I
set the account up. Email that to me as well
if you would. Thanks again and have a great
week.
```

It is always good advice to keep an eye on your credit report. You have this right and you don't have to pay for that right. Anyone can request free copies of their credit reports once a year. Go to www.ftc.gov/credit or call 877-382-4357 to get more information and to see when you can make your requests. You'll stretch your monitoring if you don't ask all three credit bureaus for your reports at the same time. Stagger your requests and you'll have a good picture of your credit report activity. Do not contact the credit bureaus directly for these free annual reports. Reports are only available by calling 877-322-8228 or going to www.annualcreditreport.com. You can make your requests by phone or online, or download a form to mail your requests.

CHAPTER 3
DEALING WITH EMAIL SCAMS

Now that you've learned to recognize the top 10 email scams, what do you do once you get one of these emails?

Tips for Avoiding Email Scams

In Chapter 2, we have provided Scam Alert Clues under many of the top 10 email scams so that you can learn to recognize them as soon as they hit your in-box. Here are additional general tips which will help you recognize email scams of any sort.

1. Scam emails are often filled with poor spelling, grammar, and formatting.

Many scam emails originate from countries outside the United States and the scammers seem to have a horrible command of the English language – and seemingly no motivation to correct their mistakes. They often use templates for their emails and do not know how to customize them and correct mistakes. That's the good news. They are easy to spot because they can be so poorly constructed. The bad news is even with this level of incompetence, they still seem to successfully get so many victims.

2. Watch out for emails coming from web-based email services.

Scammers need to hijack other people's servers in order to send out their massive mailings and they need to create temporary, disposable email accounts to receive replies – accounts that can be easily abandoned and not traced. That is why scam email addresses almost always come from services like Gmail.com, Yahoo.com, Hotmail.com, Live.com and other such services where it is free to set up an email account.

Scammers will sometimes make the address in the 'From' field look legitimate but then use the 'Reply-To' field to put their disposable email address so that when users hit Reply, it goes to them at the 'Reply-To' address.

It is also common to see scammer email addresses contain numbers. This makes it easy for a scammer to maintain a certain fake identity a little longer. If the email account gets shut down, they just open another one with a slightly different number. You might see variations of davidhoward34@gmail.com, davidhoward35@gmail.com, davidhoward45@gmail.com, etc. If all these get shut down, the scammer just makes up a new fake name and starts the numbers game all over. That is why it is so hard for Google or Yahoo or Microsoft to stay on top of shutting these types of accounts down.

3. Scammers love to send fraudulent checks and ask you to forward some of it elsewhere via wire transfer.

This is very popular in the scams involving check cashing and overpaying on an item for sale. It is typically money orders that have been counterfeited to look real. Sometimes the scammer includes documents of authorization from the United States Postal Service (the USPS doesn't provide such a document). And always is for more than the amount expected with a request to forward the difference some place else – ALWAYS via wire transfer, like Western Union. The stories vary but the process is the same.

4. Watch out for online credit card payments.

As scammers realized potential victims were becoming wise to the fake money orders, they have increasingly switched to using stolen credit card numbers. Here is the catch: they try and use stolen numbers that have not yet been reported so the number often clears but will always later result in a chargeback. Of course, this is too late for the victim who, thinking the card cleared, already forwarded the money 'difference' to a third-party (which ends up being the scammer themselves) via Western Union.

I have messed with scammers and said the credit card number didn't clear. In the meantime, I reported the number to the credit card company to take that one number out of circulation. The scammer would then quickly give me another and I would report that one as well. I've done this up to 5 numbers with a single scammer, though most give up after giving me three numbers.

5. Just decide to commit yourself to never use wire transfers in your online dealings.

My advice here is simple. Do NOT do wire transfers. Period. No Western Union, no MoneyGram. Don't accept wire transfers as any part of a transaction (especially you forwarding extra money via wire transfer) and you'll avoid a lot of purchase-related and check-cashing email scams.

6. Watch out for links in email.

The goal of a phishing scammer is to get you to click on a link in an email that you think is real but actually goes to a bogus look-alike page, usually to collect passwords or sensitive financial information.

I never click on a link in an email. I first pass my mouse over it without clicking to see if I can see where it goes. If I can't see, I'll open a new browser window and log into the website of that company and see if I can find what they are talking about independent of the email. If I can't and I just don't know how to verify that link in the email, I'll actually just not take the risk to click on it and pass it by. In one banking situation where there seem to be too many details for it to be a scam, instead of clicking on the link in the email, I called the bank on the phone and they did verify it was a legitimate email from them.

7. Look for common scam phrases in email.

This won't cover all scam emails but so many of them have common key phrases that will identify them as scams. Be on the lookout for the popular ones:

"I work for a recently deceased wealthy client" --- 419 scam

"From Dr. Mrs. Mariam Abacha" --- 419 scam

"Urgent Attention" --- phishing scam

"Read and Reply As Soon As Possible" --- phishing attack

"We have detected an unusual amount of login attempts" --- phishing scam

"Attached is the shipping invoice" --- malware scam

"Print out the attached invoice copy" --- malware scam

"The delivery of your order was unsuccessful" --- malware scam

"The parcel was undelivered" --- malware scam

"Please update your records" --- phishing scam

"We are implementing a new login/security system" --- phishing scam

"Please verify your Account" [details] --- phishing scam

"Your account has been compromised" --- phishing scam

"Problem with your account" --- phishing scam

"Please confirm your identity" --- phishing scam

"If you don't respond within 48 hours, your account will be closed " --- phishing scam

"Click the link below to gain access to your account" --- phishing scam

"You are the beneficiary to..." --- 419 scam

"Payment Agent Needed" --- check cashing scam

"Congratulations, you are the lottery winner" --- 419 scam

"Get your free upgrade now" --- malware scam

"You have been sent an e-card" --- malware scam

8. Do NOT click on email attachments unless you really know what you are clicking on.

This is the strategy for downloading viruses and malware

to your computer. Only open attachments once you know who the sender is and you are sure that person's account was not hacked and is now automatically sending out emails with dangerous attachments.

9. Watch out for urgency or pressure in an email.

Scammers rely upon getting the victim to act before they (or a banking institution or credit card company) figure out it is a scam. So it is important that a scammer create a sense of urgency in their "story". This is almost always a flag that it is a scam. Email users should never act hastily, and be aware of emails that claim you must click links, forward money, or download attachments "before it's too late" or "as soon as possible".

10. Search online before sending money or items.

It helps to search on key phrases in the email to see if others have received this or a similar email. Even though scammers fake their name and use disposable email accounts, search on these to see if others have received a similar thing. If it mentions a shipping company, search on that name. Search on any phone numbers listed.

And then share the email you've received online so it can be there in the search results when others do their search. Send it to our Blog (ktmobooks.com/blog/) or post it to the Facebook page (facebook.com/ktmobooks/). Post it to your own blog or other scam-reporting websites on the

Internet.

What To Do If You Have Been Scammed

My heart sinks every time I receive an email from someone who has actually sent money to a scammer. I hate it. And if you think this doesn't happen much, you should see my in-box! I don't want my readers to reach this point—of actually becoming a victim, but if you do suddenly find yourself in this situation, there are some steps you should take.

First of all, get over being ashamed or embarrassed. Anyone can become a victim of a scam, and I mean anyone. It is NOT a reflection of your intelligence. If you want to feel better, here is a good story for you. A real story:

> "Attention filthy rich LA Lakers fans -- Lamar Odom does not have a cash-strapped assistant ... something director Penny Marshall learned after getting jacked for several thousand bucks.
>
> Sources say the double-cross started at a Lakers game last month ... when a man claiming to be Odom's assistant gave Penny a phone number he said was Lamar's.
>
> We're told Penny and the person she thought was Lamar texted back and forth for several days -- when finally "Lamar" asked her to loan his assistant a chunk of cash. Ever the

> faithful Lakers fan, Penny forked over more than five grand to the faux "assistant."
>
> Hook. Line. Sinker.
>
> After that, we're told "Lamar" suddenly stopped texting, Penny got suspicious, and contacted the real Lamar ... who told her he doesn't even have an assistant.
>
> Penny has filed a police report with the LAPD, and we're told they've opened a grand theft investigation. Penny's rep had no comment."

Don't get sad—get MAD! Report the scam! Share it online so others see it in search results! No more hiding. I'm not saying you'll get your money back but you'll feel better letting all the proper authorities know this is a real problem and is a crime.

Keep in mind there is no point in contacting the authorities if there is no financial loss. Just receiving a scam email does not constitute a crime. It is a crime if the scammer has sent a fraudulent money order via the postal service but that is why most scammers use FedEx. FedEx doesn't really follow-up on this activity. Even if you experience financial loss, I have seen that many authorities just don't have the resources to pursue cases for small losses. And the scammers are counting on that as well. But I feel filing a report is always a good thing, so that the authorities know the scope of what is happening in their district (as well as the federal authorities).

Here are some steps you can take after you have fallen

victim to a scam:

Step 1. Do not panic.

Or, if you must, allow yourself x amount of time to panic and then get down to business. This is actually not about you anymore. That part of the experience has happened and is over. Now it is about notifying as many authorities as you can to expose the scammer. Take a moment to realize this is just one experience in many experiences in your life, good and bad, and there is no reason for this to ruin your life. Remember the old saying, it is just "stuff" and those we love are much more important. Make a list of all your blessings. Write it down. Even if you are still feeling ashamed or embarrassed—write a list of your blessings and make the list as long as you possibly can. Work on the list every day. If it helps, talk about your experience being scammed with trusted friends, family, a trusted clergy member or therapist. Talking about your loss with someone you trust is therapeutic and will help to alleviate the stress you are feeling. It will also help to offset some of the stigma, embarrassment and guilt associated with these types of crimes. Remember, you are the victim—it is NOT your fault! And scammers target everyone. They do not discriminate.

Step 2. Create an inventory list of what you have lost.

Calculate the dollar amount you have lost. Separately

include phone calls and any mail or shipping costs you may have incurred. List all items you may have lost as a result of the scam and give an estimate of their value. Collect up any documentation of real value you may have for these items.

Step 3. Detail and document the transaction.

To the best of your ability, detail exactly what happened from the first contact to the last. Write a chronological accounting of each event from beginning to end. Include any statements, emails, phone calls and if there was anything sent via mail. Print out all the emails sent and received (view the email's full headers or "source" before printing, to show the full path of where the email came from). Write everything the scammer said to you and list separately even what you thought they meant by what the scammer said. Print website screen-shots if they were involved in the scam. Think about what the authorities might ask you upon hearing your story and practice your answers. Make duplicate copies of everything. Store at least one copy in a safe location where only you have access and will not need it.

Step 4. Time to contact the proper authorities.

Scams are illegal. It is completely annoying that scammers hide in foreign countries and are difficult for the authorities to catch them. In most cases, you can not reasonably expect to receive the appropriate compensation or justice to be done to those who have hurt you, even though a crime has been committed. But I think you still must report it, to help the authorities understand the pattern and scope of the problem, and in some cases, they actually are able to do something. So take the chance and report it.

Start by contacting your local police. Ask to have a crime report filed. They will want to know what happened and how much financial loss you experienced. The police won't be able to do much but the documentation of a police report can be added to your file.

Next go on the Better Business Bureau (BBB.org) website. They can't do anything legally about your situation but they might have good advice and also they are good about spreading the words about scams.

Now, if the scammer located within a U.S. state, contact that state's Attorney General. What is more likely to be true is the scammer is hiding in a foreign country where they can not be pursued easily. In that case, contact your own State Attorney. Get their input and advice on what to do next and who to turn to. Tell them you have documentation and can provide that to them if they think it will help.

If your scammer is hiding in a foreign country, and as we

mentioned, that is likely the case, it is really important to contact the FBI, the SEC, and the FTC. Online frauds and scams have been increasing exponentially and each of these agencies have a department tasked to handle these cases. Go to the website at https://www.ic3.gov/ - this is a partnership between the Federal Bureau of Investigation and the National White Collar Crime Center. They have a form to fill out where you can describe in detail the scope, the size of the scam, and all the detailed information you have. Remember, these are federal agencies and, as such, are typically very busy, but they do eventually reply and they do work on cases where a lot of victims have entered complaints. They look at trends. Still, reporting it is important. If none of us report it, they will never know the scope of the problem.

Your local attorney. A local attorney may be able to at least refer you to the resources you need and advise you on how to proceed. If you can afford their help, it may serve you to seek their assistance. Again, the scammer may be hiding in a foreign country outside the jurisdiction of our authorities but an attorney will know this for sure.

Step 5. Repeat.

This will probably grind you down but if nothing much seems to be happening, start with step one again—the local police and ask them how their investigation is progressing. Continue with each step until you feel some progress is being made. Or you've been told with all certainty that nothing can be done.

Step 6. Post your experiences online.

Now take to the internet and post your experiences online. If you have a blog, post about it and include the actual emails, the scammer fake name and disposable email address, any shipping addresses they provide, any screenshots and web addresses involve—post everything you can, so when others search on their scam email, your experiences will come up in the search results and at least you will save a lot of other people from what you have had to go through. Go to KTMObooks Blog (ktmobooks.com/blog/), KTMObooks Facebook (facebook.com/ktmobooks), StopArtScams Blog and to Stop Art Scams Facebook (even if it is not about art) and post your experiences.

My goal is to encourage two main behaviors:

1. to have people post everything about scammers online so it becomes part of the "public" record and shows up in search results.

2. to educate people to search online BEFORE sending money to anyone but especially people they don't know.

With these steps, you should be able to feel some reassurance that you have done everything possible to rectify your situation. Then let it go. The nature of these types of crimes make it unlikely that you will recover your money or property. Life goes on. You have your life and you'll recover from your losses.

Dealing with Identity Theft

Identity theft is a special kind of scam, one that is much more devastating to the victim because of how it destroys your credit and screws up all the ways the government agencies know you are a real person and that you are you. It can take a long time to undo the damage. If you think your identity may have been stolen, here is what to do now (note: keep a log of all conversations with authorities and financial entities):

Step 1. *File a police report.* When you have discovered someone is using your identity, immediately report the crime to the police. Make sure you receive a copy of the report because your creditors may require proof of the crime.

Step 2. *Contact your bank.* Do not delay on contacting your bank if you suspect your account has or can be tampered with by an identity thief. Ask the bank to review your account for unusual activity and determine if you should close the account and open a new account with a new ID number.

Step 3. *Contact a credit bureau.* You need to place a fraud alert on your credit file and do that right away. Report the theft of your credit card(s), even if it is just the numbers online. Ask for your accounts to be flagged. Request to add your own victim's statement to your report. When a fraud alert has been placed on your account, creditors will contact you before opening any new accounts with them or before making any changes to your existing accounts with their company. The good news is you just have to contact one credit bureau. Once the one bureau makes the changes, the other two credit bureaus will be automatically be notified to place fraud alerts on your account. All three credit reports will be sent to you free of charge. Each will work with you to correct unauthorized transactions in your accounts and correct any incorrect reports, as well as help to protect you from any future identity theft or account fraud.

Step 4. *Contact your credit card issuer(s) immediately.* Your credit card issuing companies will close your credit card number(s) and send you new card(s).

Step 5. *Obtain new identity documents*. If you feel the identity thief has and/or is making use of your passport number, driver's license or other government documents, you'll need to go through the steps to obtain new ones. Explain to each agency what happened so that a new number can be assigned to you and new documents sent.

Step 6. Check all your accounts for unauthorized charges, and immediately *close the accounts* where you believe tampering can or has happened or any accounts opened fraudulently.

Step 7. *File your complaint with the FTC* (Federal Trade Commission). Visit http://www.ftc.gov/ or call the FTC's identity theft hotline toll-free at 1 (877) IDTHEFT or (877)-438-4338. They have a special section on their website for identity theft. They add information to database that law enforcement agencies access. Filing a complaint also helps them learn more about the patterns of identity theft and the problems victims experience so that they can better assist future victims.

Step 8. *Fill out the FTC identity theft affidavit.* This will assist you in reporting to many different companies that a new account has been open in your name as you rebuild your identity. Use the ID Theft Affidavit when disputing new unauthorized accounts.

Step 9. *Contact your state attorney general,* just to alert them to the scam or fraud activity, so they can monitor the crime happening in their jurisdiction.

CONCLUSION

Now that you are familiar with the top 10 most prevalent email scams, I hope you feel better equipped to handle anything scammers throw at you. To recap:

- most email scams are not new, they are just updated variations of old offline scams. The Internet has just given the scammer a larger audience at no cost to them.

- all scams contain a "story", a "target" (or "mark"), a get-in-get-out quick process, and an untraceable way to collect your money and disappear.

- it is okay to check out the details of the email before acting on it. Do not allow yourself to be rushed. Call the bank on the phone and/or search online to see if others have gotten a similar email.

- Do NOT forward your money to any third-party (especially via wire transfer), thinking you are helping someone out. Just don't do it.

- Do not give out your financial information or passwords unless you have double-checked and triple-checked via other methods (like the phone).

- Once you know it is a scam, delete the email and just

move on – no need to write to the scammer and let him know that you know. They don't care and you are just saving them time so they know to move on to the next victim. Just ignore all their communications. They don't deserve any more of your time.

- Share your scam emails online so when others search, they will benefit from your experience and know something is a scam before they become a victim. Even though scammers use fake names and disposable email addresses, they send to millions, so post it and help save someone else.

My best advice to you is this: when something doesn't feel right, don't override your gut feeling—LISTEN to it. It is okay to say 'NO' to people. Really. It is always possible to say yes later after checking multiple sources to verify the information BEFORE sending money to anyone for any reason. The old adage *if it seems too good to be true, it probably is* really fits here and there is likely a scammer behind it trying to draw you in. Trust your instincts. Don't become a scam victim and don't let the scammers outsmart you!

INTERNET SCAMS REVEALED

This book is Volume 1, the first in a short series of books covering the topic of Internet Scams. Here are the additional books in this series:

Volume 2: Social Media Scams

So many people are on social media today, and as you might expect, so are the scammers. In Volume 2, I take a more in-depth look at scams in operation on: Craigslist, Facebook, eBay, Twitter, and Pinterest.

Supplemental Resource: Report Scams

I wanted to bring together a resource of links and agencies so that victims of Internet scam can know where to turn and get help. There are listings for government agencies, non-profit organizations, where to report email scams and where to report social media abuse. This guide also has a few tips on protecting yourself online.

Check out the full book title list at KTMObooks.com.

GLOSSARY OF TERMS

4

419 Scam

Also called the Nigerian 419 Scam, this is a scam of the advanced fee fraud type and one of the most common schemes online whose main goal is monetary gain.

A

Account Takeover

The bank account, email account, social media account, utilities, or online shopping account of a victim is taken over and used. When a financial account takeover has happened, funds are removed from account(s) either by Direct Debit, payments or transfers being set up without the victim's consent.

Adware

Advertising-supported software (referred to as adware), is any software package which has advertisements automatically embedded within the software. They can be pop-up ads or in the software user interface or presented to the user during the install process. The goal is for the advertisements to generate revenue for the author of the software, which by itself is not harmful (if not annoying) but some adware comes bundled with malicious spyware that will track your keystrokes or do other damaging things to your computer.

Advanced Fee Fraud

Advanced Fee Fraud is a successful and very common online scam in which the scammer requests an upfront fee from the victim on the promise of receiving things that never come, like lottery winnings, a loan, money from a non-existent dead relative, etc.

Anti-Fraud Bureaus

State operated anti-fraud bureaus are organized to detect and investigate insurance frauds of many types. Some bureaus have a broad investigation mission, others focus on specific types of fraud, such as worker's compensation.

Anti-Virus Software

Anti-virus software is software installed on a computer to prevent, detect and remove all types of malicious software that may get installed without the user's knowledge or permission. Examples of these malicious softwares may include computer viruses, keyloggers, spyware, torjan horses, worms, adware, backdoors, malicious BHOs, dialers, hijackers, malicious LSPs, and rootkits.

Application Fraud

Application fraud involved a person applying for credit or driver's license using someone else's details or false supporting documentation.

B

Bayesian Filtering

Bayesian Filtering is a statistical approach used to determine if an email is spam.

Benefit Fraud

A crime that occurs when a person received benefits dishonestly in someone else's name.

Bin Raiding

This is when a thief or scammer rifles through household or commercial garbage bins to locate documents that might contain personal or financial account information which then might be used for identity theft.

Blind Trust

A blind trust is a trust in which trustees or those who have been given power of attorney, have full discretion over the assets, and the beneficiaries have no knowledge of the holdings of the trust and no right to intervene.

Blocked Funds

A term used when one bank reserves funds for the benefit of another bank, typically to ensure those funds are not accounted for or used twice.

Browser

A browser is a software application on a computer that allows a person to view content on the Internet visually. Examples of browsers are: Internet Explorer, Firefox, Safari and Chrome.

Browser Hijacker

This is a malware software, spyware or virus that takes the home page, error page, or search page of someone's website and replaces it with their own, typically to gain advertising fees from someone else's traffic or just to be malicious.

Bull

An investor who makes a profit from their securities when prices rise.

C

CAN-SPAM Act

The CAN-SPAM Act (Controlling the Assault of Non-Solicited Pornography And Marketing Act of 2003), a law passed by Congress and signed by President Bush in 2003, requires national standards for sending commercial emails.

This act requires email marketers to include the following in email messages:

- The subject line must clearly communicate the content

included in the body of the email.

- Emails cannot contain misleading "From" or "To" information. Domain names, email addresses and routing information needs to be correct.

- Customers must have a way to "unsubscribe" or "opt-out" from receiving messages. The company has 10 days to stop sending emails to a person who has requested an unsubscribe. This unsubscribe option needs to be available for at least 30 days after the initial email is sent.

- All commercial emails must include a physical address.

It would appear there isn't much enforcement of this law.

Card Capture Device / Card Trapping

A device that captures data contained on cards inserted into the card slot of a cash machine (ATM).

Card Cloning or 'Skimming'

Card Cloning happens when a card's magnetic stripe is read electronically by a 'skimming' device and downloaded onto a computer or copied to a duplicate card. This method is one common way thieves collect stolen credit card numbers.

Car Lease Fraud

This is when a car lease is fraudulently applied for in a victim's name.

Cashiers Check (or Cheque)

A cashier's check (also referred to as money order, cashier's cheque, bank cheque , banker's cheque, teller's cheque , official cheque, demand draft, bank draft or treasurer's cheque) is a check that is guaranteed by a bank. A chasier's check is treated as guaranteed funds and usually cleared the next business day. Banks are permitted to take back money from a "cleared" check one or two weeks later if subsequent processing finds it to be fraudulent. Because customers believe the checks have been found valid and have been converted to cash in hand, customers are frequently defrauded by scams that ask them to part with goods or a portion of the money if it is cleared in a timely manner. (See Fake Buyer Scam)

Catalogue/Store Card Fraud

This scam works one of two ways – a person receives goods they never ordered (signifying a scammer used their mailing address when attempting to get another victim to forward them money) or a person is charged for goods they never ordered or received (signifying a scammer is using their credit card).

Change of Address Fraud

A criminal will contact banks and businesses to register a change of address, using the victim's information. The crook can then order valuable items such as check books, debit cards or account statements to be sent to the new address. This is also a step used when facilitating an account takeover.

CNP (Cardholder Not Present) Fraud

This is when a scammer can purchase goods or services online, by phone, or by mail order using a stolen credit card number and not be present to show the card.

Commercial / Corporate Identity Theft

This is a type of fraud that makes use of the identity of a company, business or its directors, without their knowledge.

Commission

The fee a broker collects for dealing in their behalf.

Contract Exit for Non-Performance

A condition of a financial agreement in which the investor can take back his funds if the result represented is not achieved.

Contract Note

The date set that a transaction takes place, the broker sends a document detailing the deal to the client which itemizes the full title of the stock and price.

Cookies

A small text file that is created on your computer's hard drive to collect information about your activities on a website.

Counterfeit Card

An unauthorized reproduction of a credit or debit card, or one that has been altered.

Credit Risk

The calculation of the probability of loss in a financial loan relationship.

CSS Spam

The exploitation of Cascading Style Sheets (CSS), which control the display of web pages, used in order to conceal messages in email spam. Also used trick spam filters.

Current Address Fraud

This is an identity fraud typically perpetrated by a criminal who shares the same address as the victim, and often happens to the elderly.

Cyber Fraud

A broad term used to describe fraud activity that occurs on the Internet.

D

Day of the Jackal Fraud

This fraud involved the use of a dead child's birth certificate, many years after their death when they would have been an adult, to assume that child's adult identity and obtain a passport for purposes of identity fraud. It is so-named because of its detailed description given in Frederick Forsyth's novel.

Denial of Service (DoS) Attack

A DoS attack involves saturating a target computer server with so many simultaneous communications requests that the computer is no longer available for it's intended users.

Dictionary Attack

A dictionary attack uses a pre-arranged list of username and password values and then successively tries all the words in that list in order to break into accounts. Generally, dictionary attacks are successful because people tend to use simple password so they can remember them. Dictionary attacks can be simple to defeat, just by adding a single random character in the middle of a password can make dictionary attacks untenable.

Directory Harvest Attack (DHA)

A Directory Harvest Attack or DHA is when a spammer attempts to find valid email addresses at a given domain by using different permutations of common usernames. These attacks tend to be more effective for finding email addresses of companies since they commonly have standard formats (i.e. jsmith@example.domain, janes@example.domain, or janesmith@example.domain).

Domain Name System Block Lists (DNSBL)

A DNS-based Block List (DNSBL) or Real-time Block List (RBL) is a database of IP addresses known to be linked to spamming. Companies make use of this list in their spam filters. The term "block list" is sometimes interchanged with the terms "blacklist" and "blackhole".

Drive-by Download

This happens when deceptive popup windows appear and trick the user into thinking their computer system has an error. Often the popup error window will say to click and download a fix. Often then software or possibly even a virus gets downloaded and the vendor claims the user “consented” because they clicked on the link.

Drop Box

Also referred to as Mail Drop, Throwaway Account, or Disposable Account, these accounts are used by a spammers for the purpose of receiving replies to their spams. These accounts are expendable as they lose them frequently are typically found at free email providers who require minimal information or verification.

E

Encryption

Encryption is a process that takes readable information and makes it unreadable to anyone except those possessing the "key", which unlocks it (called decryption).

F

False Negative

An email filtering program will generate a false negative when it identifies an email as "safe" and not spam when it is, in fact, spam.

False Positive

An email filtering program will generate a false positive when it identifies an email as spam and not "safe" when it is, in fact, safe.

Firewall

Computer hardware or software that is used to keep a network secure. It controls the incoming and outgoing network traffic by analyzing data packets and determining whether it should be allowed through or not, based on a preconfigured rule set.

First Party Fraud

Fraud that is committed against a financial institution by one of its own customers.

Flooding

Flooding is when a large numbers of messages is sent to a single newsgroup or forum, either as a mistake from a newbie, or as deliberate act. Also known as Vertical Spam.

Fudiciary Officer

The word "fiduciary" is misspelled. Scammers frequently misspell this word in their scams. No legitimate company makes this mistake.

G

Greylist

Greylist describes a technique for blocking spam based on the behavior of the sending server rather than the content of the messages.

H

Hacker

This is a term used to describe someone who purposely breaks through computer security systems. They typically so it in order to get information or just to demonstrate that it can be done. Scammers will "hack" into someone's email account in order to send spam out of their account. Or they might steal credit card numbers by "hacking" into the secured systems of a large commerce company.

Ham

This refers to automatic spam filters that can classify email as either spam or ham (i.e. not spam).

Hardcover Insurance Policy

There is no such thing as a hardcover insurance policy. Scammers make this up in order to trick victims into believing there is some policy for which they must pay an extra fee.

Harvesting

The process spammers and scammers use to automatically search webpages and other online documents with software looking for email addresses to collect and then send spam emails to.

Hash Buster

Hash Buster is a method spammers use to avoid getting their spam mail caught by spam filters. This method inserts randomly generated content in each spam mail, confusing the filtering software which looks for identical messages, because each wave of spam appear unique and individual to the filter.

Honeypot

An Internet-server which acts as a decoy to lure in potential hackers in order to study and monitor how they break into a system.

I

Identity Fraud / Theft

The use of a person's identifying details (name, date of birth, current or previous address, mother's maiden name, etc.) without their consent or knowledge in order to assume their identity.

Impersonation of the Deceased (IOD) Fraud

A criminal uses the identity of a deceased person in order to facilitate fraudulent activity (see Day of the Jackal fraud).

J

Joe Job

A joe job is a term used in the past to describe a spamming technique that would tarnish the reputation of the victim by making that email look like it was coming from them. Sometimes seen in politics. Lately, these types of emails are more just used by commercial spammers to conceal the true origin of their messages.

K

Keystroke Logger

Keystroke logging software is installed on computers, typically without the users knowledge or consent, in order to record keystrokes and mouse movements. Scammers use this in order to discover account passwords, usernames, credit card number and any other useful information.

L

Listwashing

Spammers and scammers want to make money and not waste time. Listwashing refers to the process of spammers removing "troublemakers" (those who have complained to their ISPs) so they can concentrate their efforts on people still on the list. Listwashing also refers to the legitimate process of removing people who request an unsubscribe from a mailing list. But spammers also use unsubscribe requests as a means of validating active email addresses which they can sell for more money.

Loan (unsecured) Fraud

This scam involves unsecured credit loans. Scammers will offer the loan, regardless of the victim's credit history, saying they loan to those who can't get a loan. Then they charge an upfront fee. The loan never comes through and the scammer is gone with the fee money.

Lost and Stolen Card Fraud

This is a sweet spot for scammers – they use credit card numbers that have been lost or stolen but not yet report and so the payment will clear with the vendor, but later turn out to be a chargeback, too late for the vendor.

M

Mail Bomb

This is when a huge number of and/or excessively large pieces of email are sent to a single email address all at one time or nonstop, with the aim being to prevent normal use of the mailbox. Often used by a scammer or spammer who has gotten upset with an individual or a company.

Mail Drop

Also referred to as Mail Drop, Throwaway Account, or Disposable Account, these accounts are used by a spammers for the purpose of receiving replies to their spams. These accounts are expendable as they lose them frequently are typically found at free email providers who require minimal information or verification.

Mail Loop

A mail loop is when one automated mail triggers another which triggers the first mail to reply etc., creating an endless mail loop. This causes high pressure on mail servers and slower service.

Malware

Malware, which is short for malicious software, is used by hackers to disrupt computer operations, spread viruses or worms, gather sensitive information, or gain access to private computer systems.

Man-in-the-Middle Attack

Man-In-The-Middle attack is the type of cyber attack where hackers intrude into an existing connection to intercept the exchanging data and inject into that data false information. It involves the steps of eavesdropping on a connection, hacking into a connection, intercepting messages and data packs, and selectively modifying data and sending it on it's way again.

Mail Re-direct (or Mail Re-Ship)

This is when a scammer uses the re-direct services of the post office or UPS to re-route a package to a different address, all done without the knowledge or consent of the person the package was intended for. This is often used to get bank statements and account numbers and any other information that will facilitate identity theft. It is also used to collect money, such as people's social security check.

Morph

This is when a spammer alters the email header information in order to avoid detection by anti-spam software so that their email will get through to the user.

Mousetrapping

This is an annoying technique used by annoying people who hijack other people's websites and insert their own pages. Then when visitors land on the bogus page and tries to use the back button to escape, they are only redirected to more unwanted pages and the back button never gets them back to where they were. One just has to hit the Home key and start over.

Munging

This is a technique used to alter an email address on a website so that spammer software can not detect it and collect it into their spam database. Those legitimate users who receive a 'munged' address are told how to decode it so that they can reply. There are also javascript programs that munge email addresses into what looks like random characters but when it is clicked on, it opens the users email program, decodes the email address and automatically loads it in their "TO" field.

N

NDR Spam

NDR (Non Delivery Report) spam is when a spammer will generate a fake non-delivery error message that goes to a user, who will then think one of their emails bounced back and they will be tricked into opening the attachment to see what email bounced, and the attachment will end being a virus. Sometimes spammers can even make a legitimate server send these fake notifications for them, making them seem more legitimate and harder to detect as spam.

O

Obfuscation

Another term used for when spammers hide data in order to avoid being detected as spam by spam filter programs. Also this term is used when regular users hide their email address so that spammer software can not recognize it and collect it up to spam to. (See munging)

Open Relay

An open relay server is a mail server that is unsecured and allows any email to pass through it, making it possible for spammers to send large amounts of unwanted mail and abuse through it. Often these servers end up on Blacklists and the whole server is blocked by companies, to help reduce the spam levels.

Opt-in

This is the process of a user actively choosing and agreeing to receive email from a business or group. Single opt-in when a user selects yes to receive the emails and double opt-in is when after saying yes to receiving email, the user also has to confirm they actually said yes via their own email account, to make sure no one is opting them in without their knowledge or permission.

Opt-out

This is the process of declining to receive email from a business or group or the act of unsubscribing if the person is already on the mailing list. Double opt-out asks the user to confirm one more time that they actually want to be removed.

P

Page Jacking

Page jacking involves stealing the contents of a website by copying some of its pages, placing them on a site that appears to be legitimate, and having the contents indexed by major search engines (also known as search engine spamming), so that unsuspecting users can be tricked into linking to the illegitimate pages. Typically used by spammers to generate more traffic to advertising for revenue. (see also mousetrapping.)

Password Stealer

Password stealer software is very similar to keylogger software. Keylogger software captures everything that is being typed in the hopes of discovering credit card numbers as well as passwords. Password stealer software only focuses on capturing passwords that are being typed by the user.

Pharming

"Pharming" (pronounced 'farming') is similar to page jacking in that a scammer has taken over a web page on a legitimate site and installed their own fake page in it's place. But the fake page looks almost identical to the real thing. The Scammer uses this to trick users into entering their account information and passwords. (see Phishing)

Phishing

"Phishing" (pronounced 'fishing') is when you get what seems to be a legit email inviting you to click a link that takes you to a website that also looks genuine. But you never arrive at the legitimate website. Instead, you end up at a URL that is slightly (or not even slightly) different than the legitimate one. The page at the bogus site looks almost identical to the legitimate one. Users not paying attention may not even notice and proceed to enter their account information and password. (see Pharming; Spy Phishing)

Phreaking

This is not specifically Internet related but a common hacking term. It involves criminals illegally breaking into the telephone network to make free long-distance phone calls or to tap phone lines. This term is also used to include the act of breaching the security of any network, including the Internet.

R

Ratware

Spammers like to be efficient, too. So they have software, called ratware, which helps them automate spam campaigns, coordinate spam services, and generate, send and track spam messages.

Real-time Block List (RBL)

RBLs are a little different than block lists in that it dynamically boycotts TCP/IP addresses known to send spam or host spammers. Enabling such a list results in ALL mail from those addresses being refused, including legitimate email. Users can experience difficulty receiving email and not know why and their ISP (Internet Service Provider) may have been added to one of these lists. Then the ISP has to enact stronger anti-spam measures to get removed from the RBL list.

S

Second Party Fraud

Fraud that is committed by someone close to or known by the victim, usually a relative or employee. (see First Party Fraud)

Shoulder Surfing

This is what is referred to when someone looks over someone else's shoulder at a cash machine, making payments or filling out an application form in order to capture personal details and PIN numbers to facilitate identity fraud.

Skimmer

A device that reads and records details held on the magnetic stripe of payment cards.

Social Engineering Scams

This is when a scam uses people's natural tendency to respect authorities and their basic willingness to help others and exploit those tendencies in order to operate their scams. Most successful scams contain this exploitation.

Sock Puppet

A sockpuppet is an online identity used for purposes of deception. Previously, a sock puppet would be when one person created a false identity online in order to trash someone else or a company. Now it's just used when someone creates an online personality in order to pretend to be other than themselves. Forums used to call them Trolls – they would create an identity and then stir up controversy just to see people get upset. Companies also create sock puppet identities in order to make it look like people love their product.

Spambait

Spambait is when purposely invalid email addresses that are planted on a website with the expectations that they will be harvested by a spambot and thereby pollute their database with bad email addresses. It is also possible to place "bait" that trap spambots in endless loops or generate large amounts of invalid email addresses to counterstrike spammers even more.

Spambot

A program that spammers use to harvest email addresses from the Internet.

Spam Trap

Spam trap is an email address specifically set up for the purpose of capturing unsolicited email spams for the purpose of tracking the spammers. The spam trap term is also used to refer to an option on an online form that is pre-selected by default, so unwary users opt-in to receive spam.

Spim

When a spam occurs by instant messaging like Skype or ICQ, it is known and 'spim'.

Sping

Sping is shortened term for "spam ping", and is related to blogs that use “trackbacks”, so these spam are also known as “trackback spam”.Pings go from a blog to a centralized network service (a ping server) providing notification of newly published blog posts. Spings, or ping spam, are pings that are sent from spam blogs, or are sometimes multiple pings in a short interval from a legitimate source, often tens or hundreds per minute, due to misconfigured software, or a wish to make the content coming from the source appear fresh and important.

SPIT Spam

SPIT (SPam over Internet Telephony) is similar to email spam but happens with automatically dialled, pre-recorded phone calls over Voice over Internet Protocol (VoIP), on services such as Skype. It is similar to email spam. It is also referred to as VoIP Spam. A VoIP spammer is referred to as a 'spitter'. (see VoIP Spam)

Splog

A splog (spam blog) is a blog which the author uses to fill up with revenue-generating affiliated websites links, to increase the search engine rankings of associated sites or to simply sell links/ads. Spam blogs are usually a type of scraper site, where content is often either inauthentic text or merely stolen from other websites. These blogs usually contain a high number of links to sites associated with the creator which are often disreputable or otherwise useless websites but have lots of ads on them.

Spoofing

Spoofing is when spammers alter the email headers to hide the real origin of a spam email message. Email scammers and virus writers also use this trick. Scammers spoof address lines to fool people into thinking an email has arrived from a legitimate source, such as an online bank. Similarly, virus writers have passed off viruses as security patches by spoofing their origin as being, for example, from Microsoft technical support.

Spy-Phishing

In Phishing ('fishing'), the scammer gets the victim to a fake look-alike page and tricks them into entering sensitive information and passwords. In Spy Phishing, trojan and/or spyware software is downloaded onto a computer and the user doesn't have to be at a fake website, the spy software just monitors what the user is doing to silently discover identity and financial information. It then sends that information back to the scammer. This type of phishing is also well suited to government and corporate espionage.

Spyware

A software program that may be installed on your computer without your permission or knowledge to monitor your use, send pop-up ads, send your computer to certain websites, or record keystrokes, which could lead to identity theft.

T

Tarpitting

A tarpit (also known as Teergrube, the German word for tarpit) is a computer server which is delaying incoming connections for as long as possible. The technique is a defense when a server is under attack from a worm. The concept is if the work will be less effective if everything it needs to do takes a really long time from the server. (see Teergrube)

Teergrube

Teergrube (the German word for tarpit) is the same as tarpitting, slowing the services on a server down so that worms and spamming can be less effective. (see Tarpitting)

Third Party Fraud

Fraud committed against an organization or individual by an unrelated or unknown third party.

Tricklers

Tricklers are small hidden programs that basically automatically re-install malware and viruses which have been removed from a computer. If you remove the virus but not the trickler, the next time you turn on your computer, it will re-install itself again. These are most often used to silently re-install spyware so that monitoring of a computer can continue.

Trojan Horse

A trojan horse is software that gets installed on a computer without the user's knowledge or consent and it's sole purpose is to counteract the security system of a computer or network and leave a "door" open for hackers to enter the system.

U

Utility Fraud

Utilities or services are billed to the victim that the victim is not using.

V

VoIP Spam

VoIP spam is unwanted, pre-recorded, automatically dialled, phone calls using Voice over Internet Protocol (VoIP), on services such as Skype. It is similar to email spam. It is sometimes referred to by the acronym SPIT (SPam over Internet Telephony). A VoIP spammer is referred to as a 'spitter'. (see SPIT Spam)

W

Web Bug

A small graphic, sometimes just a graphical dot, added in an email or web page that alerts a spammer when a message is read or previewed.

Whack-a-Mole

An endearing phrase referring to the practice of repeatedly causing spammer's throwaway accounts and drop boxes to be terminated. Also affectionately known as "KILLS".

Worm

A program that installs on a computer without the user's knowledge or permission, reproduces itself over a network, spreads itself out over many computers on the Intenet, and can use up computer resources and possibly shut your system down.

Z

Zombie

An unsecured web server or computer that is hijacked without the owner's knowledge in order to silently used it's resources in a DoS attack on other computers or to send spam.

ABOUT THE AUTHOR

Kathleen McMahon has expertise and knowledge built upon 30 years in the hi-tech industry, including 18 years as an Internet business owner. Kathleen launched one of the first art-related websites on the Internet in 1994 and in 1995 she authored the book, "*In Search of Arts & Crafts on the Internet*". She co-founded a successful Internet advertising agency for 15 years and now provides Internet consulting and coaching services for small businesses.

Kathleen currently hosts active blogs and Facebook pages where users share their scam email experiences. When she's not writing, speaking, or consulting with her Internet clients, she can be found creating fine art, primarily California landscape paintings.

Kathleen has a growing collection of book titles, which can be found at KTMObooks.com.

If you enjoyed this book, feel free to post a review on Amazon.

"Fraud and falsehood only dread examination. Truth invites it." - Samuel Johnson

Made in the USA
Monee, IL
04 November 2026

67386595R00089